JOHN PAUL'S
Extraordinary Synod

JOHN PAUL'S Extraordinary Synod

A Collegial Achievement

by
Xavier Rynne

Foreword by George G. Higgins

Michael Glazier
Wilmington, Delaware

The publisher wishes to acknowledge and thank the *Long Island Catholic* for permission to use the photographs on page xii.

First published in 1986 by Michael Glazier, Inc. 1935 West Fourth Street, Wilmington, Delaware, 19805.
Library of Congress Catalog Card Number: 86-45330.
International Standard Book Number: 0-89453-601 X.
Typography by Dick Smith, Sandy Almeida.
Printed in the United States of America.

TABLE OF CONTENTS

To the Rynnes of
Clare and Kerry

"This is the chief goal of the Ecumenical Council, that the sacred deposit of Christian doctrine be better observed and presented. This doctrine regards the whole man, body and soul. The doctrine orders us who are citizens of earth to tend as pilgrims to the heavenly fatherland. It also shows how this mortal life is to be composed with that other one, so that fulfilling the duties which flow to us from our dual citizenship we can attain the goal set for us by God... That this doctrine may influence all spheres of activity, individuals, family life, social life, it is necessary that the Church never turn its eyes from the sacred patrimony of truth received from the Fathers. The Church must keep in mind new situations, new forms of life that open up new ways for the Catholic apostolate... ours is not just the task of guarding this sacred treasure as if it were a museum piece, but to apply it fearlessly, courageously to the needs of our time..."

Discourse of Pope John XXIII
Inaugurating Vatican Council II
October 11, 1962

Foreword

We have all had the experience of being suddenly taken aback on reading in the daily press the obituary of a famous citizen who had been out of the news so long that we thought he had been dead for years. I had the opposite experience on receiving the page proofs of Xavier Rynne's Report on the 1985 Extraordinary Synod of Bishops. Not having heard of Rynne for many years, I assumed that he had long since gone to wherever it is that "insider" journalists of his stripe are committed or consigned when the Angel of Death taps them on the shoulder and informs them that their time is up. It came as a pleasant surprise, then, to learn that I was wrong about that— that Xavier Rynne, praise the Lord, is still among the living and still going strong. He has mellowed a bit, as humans are prone to do in their later years, but, basically, he is still the same zestful and well informed reporter and analyst who served us all so well with his first series of *Letters from Rome*, published in *The New Yorker* before and during Vatican II.

Rynne's identity, of course, remains a mystery, at least so far as the public record is concerned. During the past twenty years a number of diligent sleuths have tried to unravel this mystery and some even claim to have succeeded in doing so. One example sticks in my memory for obvious reasons. Some years ago, A.J. Matt, Jr., Editor of *The Wanderer*, informed his readers, in a burst of overconfidence, that the writer of this Introduction was the real Xavier Rynne. That aroused my suspicion, and, having carefully reviewed all the evidence a la Sherlock Holmes, I concluded that Mr. Matt himself was the real Xavier Rynne, my logic being that pinning the name (and, from his point of view, the blame) on me was simply a diversionary ploy on his part designed to cover his own tracks and to throw his readers off the scent. I was only jesting, of course, for every schoolboy knows that Xavier Rynne and the Editor of *The Wanderer* are not to be confused with one another. This is by way of pointing out, for present purposes, that Rynne's Report on the Synod predictably differs, and markedly so, from *The Wanderer's* account of the same event.

The book is an informative exercise in what Rynne himself terms "theological journalism." It summarizes in adequate detail the daily Synodal bulletins and briefings at the Vatican press office and also draws on a number of articles about the Synod in European publications. In addition, it quotes to good effect from several books written on the very eve of the Synod by European journalists and prelates, including, notably, a remarkable series of exceedingly frank Itailan-language interviews with Cardinal Franz Koenig, the retired Archbishop of Vienna, who played such a crucial role in Vatican II and in the conclave which elected the present Pontiff.

Rynne interprets this disparate mass of material in the light of numerous conversations he had with Synod participants, journalists, and a host of clerical and lay friends on the Roman scene. It is clear that he is not only indefatigable, but also highly ingenious in tracking down knowledgeable sources of this type and persuading them to talk very freely both on and off the record.

To round out his coverage of the Synod, Rynne analyzes its *Message to the People of God* and its *Final Report*. Both documents are reproduced, for ready reference, as appendices to the book.

Rynne disarmingly admits that, while intent on reporting without emotion or prejudice, he is aware of a certain personal bias (in his own words, a *tendenz*) "favoring the forward looking stance of a majority of the Synod prelates." To his credit, he keeps this *tendenz* under fairly tight control and succeeds in being just about as objective as either a "liberal" or "conservative" could hope to be in covering an event which many if not most of his journalistic peers gleefully predicted would turn out to be a dramatic, metaphorically bloody shoot-out at high noon between the pro-and anti-Ratzinger forces at the Synod, with the Holy Father siding with the former. The fact that their dire predictions, which in some cases were probably the product of wishful thinking on their part, proved to be largely unfounded, was a source of poorly concealed disappointment and chagrin to a number of the less experienced and less sophisticated scribes, but that's neither here nor there.

Rynne is critical of the Synod in certain respects, but never harshly so. Pre-publication advertisements of his book were on target when they said that it "gives us an informative and balanced appraisal of the theological achievement of the Synod, where it became surprisingly obvious that the epicentre of Catholicism had shifted to Africa and Asia—and a new and vibrant era had begun."

By Rynne's own admission, his book is only a partial record of what was said and done at the assembly and does not claim to be a "taxative" account of the Synod's many facets. In any event, he has put together a readable and informative interim report on the Synod, and I am pleased to recommend it.

Welcome back, Xavier Rynne. We have missed you in recent years. It is good to know that you are still on the job and that, during your period of hibernation, you have lost none of your zest for the kind of enterprising behind-the-scenes reporting that you first displayed to such good effect in your pathfinding coverage of Vatican II.

George G. Higgins
The Catholic University of America
March 25, 1986

From the Four Corners

1. Cardinal John Krol, Archbishop of Philadelphia

2. His Excellency Gregorios B. Varghese Thangalathil, Metropolitan Archbishop of Trivandrum for the Malankarese

3. Cardinal Fredrich Wetter, Archbishop of Munich and Feising

4. Archbishop Denis Hurley, Durban, South Africa

Introduction

Coincident with the inauguration of Vatican Council II on October 11, 1962, a *Letter from Vatican City* appeared in the *New Yorker*. It occasioned concern in Rome and wonderment among Catholics and others in on the literary scene. The name of the writer, Xavier Rynne, was unknown. It was presumed to be a pseudonym and eventually gave rise to a to-do among ecclesial sleuths and literary pundits. Their frustrations were captured in John Cogley's desperate verse:

> I know their habits and their next of kin
> But who the hell is Xavier Rynne[1]

The stir in the Church was occasioned by Rynne's portrayal of the skirmishing and intrigue that accompanied the preparations for Pope John XXIII's Ecumenical Council, particularly in the control exercised by the papal curia —the bureaucratic offices of the Vatican rule — over the agenda for this great event.[2]

American and British ecclesiastics in particular were stunned by the revelations of Roman prelatial chicanery whereby pressure was being put on the portly Pontiff to cancel, or at least postpone the Council; and the fact that progressive bishops and theologians from around the world

[1]Cf. "Literary Intelligence," *America*, Oct. 19, 1963.

[2]Cf. Xavier Rynne, *The First Session* (New York, 1963); G. Licheri, *Dove vai Chiesa?* (Rome, Borla, 1985) pp. 16-20.

were simply not being invited to participate in the preparation of matters to be discussed, despite Pope John's explicit command that the whole Church be involved.

Eventually, of course, John got his way. His successor, Pope Paul VI continued the Council after his revered predecessor's death on June 3, 1963; and after four two-month sessions, with its sixteen constitutions, decrees and declarations, the Council was brought to a successful conclusion on December 8, 1965.[3]

Conscious of the continued importance of the Council in the Church's life today, Pope John Paul II decided to celebrate the twentieth anniversary of that great event's conclusion with a two-week mini-Synod set to terminate on December 8, 1985 with a commemoration of the Council's close.[4]

This brief monograph on the Synod is an attempt at theological journalism, as were the original *Letters from Vatican City.* While it represents a peripheral, on-the-scene participation in the synodal events, and aspires to preserving a partial record of what was said and done at that assembly, it makes no claim to a taxative account of the Synod's many facets.

In no sense is this essay intended as a critique of the reign of the present pontiff, John Paul II. Nevertheless in the central position he holds in the Church, with the bishops as successors of the apostles surrounding Peter's successor as bishop of Rome in a concursus or college, the Synod can only be understood in the shadow of the Holy Father. He is, after all, the initiator of the Synod and the final word as to its accomplishment. Thus it would be impossible not to judge of his words and deeds *vis-à-vis* the issues that were aired at this extraordinary assembly.

One undeniable characteristic of this colloquy was the fact that it proved to be a conversation between the world's Catholic bishops with the Pope looking on, and the non-Catholic observers kibitzing to their hearts content. In that

[3]Cf. W. Abbot, J. Gallagher, *The Documents of Vatican II* (New York, 1966).

[4]F. Murphy, "Varied Goals for Bishops' Synod," *Boston Globe* 25 Feb. 1985; "A Call for Roman Catholics," *Los Angeles Times*, 10 February 1985.

sense it was a reliving of the Council.

Nor is it possible to analyze the Synod without giving consideration to the two popes, John XXIII and Paul VI, who managed the Council and gave the present pontiff a name. Whether the Synod proved to be Johannine or Pauline is a moot question. Despite the present pontiff's forbearance during the synodal discussions, it could not but have been of John Paul II.

While intent on reporting *sine ira et studio* — without emotion or prejudice — the author is well aware of a *tendenz* favoring the forward looking stance of a majority of the synodal prelates. We feel this is in keeping with Pope John's desire that the Council should supply the Church with a *piattaforma* for a *balzo in avanti* — a platform for a leap ahead under the guidance of the Holy Spirit.

Most of the material gathered here was available in Rome during the Synod from the daily bulletins and briefings in the Vatican *sala stampa* (press office) to books, magazines and periodicals, and the daily accounts in the press, particularly the Italian, English, German and French newspapers.

This account likewise represents the result of conversations with many of the prelatial participants, prandial sessions with journalists, and the opinions of clerical and lay friends in and on the Roman scene.

The opinions attributed to the various synodal particpants and observers are as accurate as the brief time for this *tour de force* allowed. Our apologies are hereby extended to whomever we may have unintentionally misrepresented.

It remains but to thank the people who aided us in our efforts to collect the material used here, and in particular the personnel of the Vatican *sala stampa*, the director of the *Libreria Leoniana*, and the various journalists and theologians whose conversations we enjoyed, the editors of the *Tablet, America* and of the Boston Globe's editorial page where articles embodied here originally appeared, the typists, and Michael Glazier for so graciously agreeing to publish this account of the Synod with all due haste.

Go little book . . .

— *Xavier Rynne*

1

How It All Began

On Thursday morning, 11 October, 1962, Pope John's second Vatican Council began with a burst of religious pageantry that capped the octogenarian pontiff's three years of anguished preparation. It caught the fancy of well over 1,000 journalists and artisans of the news media many of whom stayed in Rome to see it through its first two months of gestation.

Promptly at eight o'clock that morning, the bronze doors of the Vatican palace flanking St. Peter's basilica slowly opened. They revealed an immense phalanx of bishops resplendent in their white copes and mitres, here and there oriental prelates in black or gold vestments with rounded headdresses, red-robed clerics and black vested courtiers framed in a flood of television lights as they descended the scala regia from the court of St. Damasus, and in rows of six, wheeled across the piazza of St. Peter's and disappeared into the vast basilica. Behind them on the sedia gestatoria, looking small and timid under his dome-shaped tiara, came Pope John only gradually warming to the huzzahs of the awed crowd. As his escort mounted the scalinata leading into the basilica, tears ran down his pallid cheeks. John's council was a reality.[1]

Elected to the papacy on the third day of the 1958 con-

[1] *F. Murphy, Tablet* (London), 9 Oct. 1983, pp. 1004-05.

clave at the age of 77, John had been labelled a transitional pope. Accepting that designation as a challenge, the portly pontiff felt called upon to turn the Church upside down. In its 1,900 years it had not preached the Gospel to every creature; nor had it achieved the unity of Christians, much less mankind, that Christ had prayed for so ardently.

In summoning the council, John had seemed to do all the wrong things. When he confided word of this venture to a group of curial cardinals in St. Paul's basilica on January 25, 1959, his announcement was met with icy silence. Creating a group of his former fellow diplomats, cardinals, among them Paolo Giobbe, Fernando Cento, Carlo Chiarlo, he found them opposed to his plans.

While John had declared that the Roman Curia would have nothing to do with the council as such, he entrusted his secretary of state, Cardinal Domenico Tardini, with organising the preliminary commissions and allowed the conservative cardinal, Alfredo Ottaviani of the Holy Office, to dominate their deliberations. To man the commissions they employed prelates and professors of the Roman ecclesiastical institutions, integralists almost to a man. Under the presidency of curial cardinals, the ten preparatory commissions prepared 72 schemata bulging with textbook theology as the agenda for an assembly of over 2,000 prelates projected in terms of one or two months' duration.

Withholding invitations to prelates and theologians known for their innovative views — the retired Archbishop of Bombay, Thomas Roberts, auxilary Bishop Joseph Reuss of Mainz along with the Yves Congars, Karl Rahners and John Courtney Murrays, they took every opportunity to persuade the aging pontiff to postpone the meeting with, as a cynical prelate observed, the well known Roman hope that providence would intervene. But the more they pleaded for delay, the more John determined to advance the opening date.

Ironically, it was with the sudden death of Cardinal Tardini in July 1961, that the conciliar preparations took a more hopeful turn. With the support of prelates from the north — Montini in Milan, Lercaro in Bologna, Liénart in

France, Doepfner in Germany, Alfrink in Holland, Suenens in Belgium, Leger in Canada, Meyer and Ritter in the USA — John forced an opening for theologians and experts of a wider vision bringing to the commissions men such as Joseph Gallagher, Barnabas Ahern, Raymond Bosler, Charles Moeller, Frederick McManus, Gustav Thils, George Higgins, John Quinn, Luigi Ligutti and Gregory Baum, as well as the all-but-banished Congars, Rahners and Küngs. By the time the council opened they had managed to boil down the agenda to 17 items for conciliar discussion.

It was in his address at the Mass of the Holy Spirit inaugurating the council that John dropped a pastoral bombshell. In his sonorous Latin with majestic pauses and unmistakable emphases, he said the council had not been called to discuss one or another of the fundamental truths of the faith. They had been sufficiently refined over the ages. Rather, the council was aimed at restoring unity, first to Christians, then to the world. To achieve this aim, the Church would have to take a step forward in penetrating the consciousness of modern mankind.

While in the past, John asserted, the Church had used severity in confronting error, now it was called upon to apply the medicine of mercy. Thus the council would take on a truly pastoral tone. Dismissing the opposition of his curial counsellors as "prophets of Doom," he said they knew no history. Now, as in times past, the Church had to restate its teaching in a medium that would employ the tools of modern scholarship and technology. Then came the lapidary sentence: "The truths of the deposit of faith are one thing; how they are expressed is another."

With that assertion, many of his prelatial listeners felt the Pope was close to heresy. But to those of us teaching in Rome, and to the council generally, John's address proved to be the *magna carta* that liberated the conciliar deliberations from the domination of the Curia and the control of the ancient Holy Office.

The fruits of this papal directive appeared in the council's first working session on Saturday, 13 October. Immediately following the opening prayer — *Adsumus, Domine* — Lord, we are here — Cardinal Achille Liénart of Lille moved that the voting on the members of the ten commissions which were to be charged with reworking the conciliar documents be postponed. The delay would allow national and regional groups of conciliar bishops — there were 35 by geography and language — to select candidates of their own choice rather than the lists prepared by the Curia. The motion was seconded immediately by Cardinal Frings of Cologne. With the acclamation of a majority of the assembly, the matter was settled.

In some consternation, Cardinal Tisserant, as president of the council, realized that there was nothing further on the day's agenda and dismissed the assembly. To the amazement of journalists and observers in the piazza of St. Peter's, cardinals, bishops and periti came tumbling out of the basilica like a group of school-boys unexpectedly released from class, and headed in buses and cars for their respective colleges and pensioni.

This delay had a two-fold effect. In a flurry of activity over the weekend, key bishops of the regional groups who knew each other from their seminary days in Rome, Louvain, Salamanca, or Innsbruck, or in chance meetings at international gatherings, made contact with each other. They established what amounted to a structure for parliamentary lobbying.

Likewise the delay betrayed a liberalising tendency among the majority of the residential bishops, a fact that greatly heartened the Pope. While he preserved his neutrality, not attending the working sessions, — observing instead on a closed-circuit TV screen — he did intervene on several occasions to untangle knotty problems such as the impasse over the schema on revelation and the insertion of the name of Joseph in the Canon of the Mass.

The freedom of the conciliar debate had been demonstrated, almost. It was to run up against the astute announcements and tortuous propositions of the magnificent Latinist and quick-witted punster, Archbishop (the late cardinal) Pericle Felici whom Cardinal Tardini bequeathed to the Council as its secretary general, a stroke of genius.

For this rotund legalist, for all his favouring the conservative cause, kept order in the assembly by his frequent jarring admonitions and jocose interjections.

In amazingly short order the Council took on a contour of its own quite different from the structure projected by the curial officials. Each day's debate was presided over by one of the 12 cardinal presidents — residential archbishops from around the globe — whose main task was to keep the speaker to the topic of the day and bell down those who abused the ten minute limit. The latter proved impossible with Cardinal Ottaviani, pro-prefect of the Holy Office, who declared himself the pope's policeman, keeping law and order in the Church's doctrine and discipline. He was visibly insulted when told to stop talking, and, in a huff, stalked out of the Council and stayed away for two weeks.

Quickly the prelates who where to predominate in the debate rose to the surface. As the discussions were conducted in Latin except by the formidable Melchite Patriarch, Maximos IV Saigh, who spoke in French as the *lingua franca* of his geographic home — cardinals and bishops with a background in European seminary teaching were at an advantage. Besides the curial cardinals, they included Siri of Genoa, Suenens of Malines, Doepfner of Munich, Leger of Montreal. Others, particularly the English speakers — with the exception of Abbot Basil Butler, a classicist — such as Godfrey of London, Spellman of New York, Gilroy of Australia and Gracias of Bombay had to rely on the expertise of their theologians in composing their interventions.

This circumstance resulted in multitudinous evening gatherings of bishops and periti in various colleges and pensioni — the English College, the Casa Maria, the Villanova — where short speeches were hammered out amid vociferous arguments, then peddled among the bishops for conciliar delivery.

Of all John's preparations, the erection of two coffee bars adjoining the water closets on each side of the basilica proved a marvellous invention. Referred to affectionately as the Bar-Jonah and the Bar-abbas, these facilities in which cardinals, bishops, periti as well as the vigili fuoco or firemen and the *sanpietrini* or Vatican workmen vied for the attention of the attendants to obtain their coffee and patisserie, while protecting themselves from the jostling crowd, provided a neutral area where opponents in the debate came face to face with one another. Here an Archbishop Heenan or Beck after a veiled sally against Bernard Häring or Hans Küng found himself confronted with these supposed heretics; and Cardinal Ottaviani, whose eyesight was failing, would be aided in getting his cappuccino by Archbishop Roberts or Abbot Butler.

It was here too that the conciliar fathers made the acquaintance of the Orthodox and Protestant observers whose presence at the council was such a significant impetus to its encouragement of the Christian unity so ardently willed by the Pope.

One result of Vatican Council II had been a revolutionary consciousness of the Church's need to cooperate with the world communications media in propagating its message. The alternative was to suffer the consequences of running scared before the merciless scrutiny of newshawks and exploratory cameras — a tendency still not totally overcome in the Roman curia.

During the Council, thanks to an assiduous siege by the secular press, the obsessive secrecy of the Church's bureaucracy was pierced.

While the discussions were conducted in strict secrecy, daily bulletins were issued by the Vatican press office and, gradually, briefings were organized in several languages for the journalists immediately after each session. Good investigative reporting resulted in leaks appearing in both the religious press — *The Tablet*, the *Month*, the *Universe*, *America*, *Etudes*, *Orientierung* and the secular dailies with Peter Nichols of the [London] *Times*, Henri Fesquet of *Le Monde*, Bill Pepper of *Newsweek*, and Giancarlo Zizzola of *II Giorno*.

When a *Letter from Vatican City* by Xavier Rynne appeared in the *New Yorker*, an enterprising peritus had copies run off in mimeograph and distributed among the

English-speaking prelates. Most of them were severely shocked on reading for the first time of the curial intrigue that accompanied the council preparations. Among Rynne's sallies was the pasquinade: "Why the conciliar secrecy?" "Because secrets travel faster."

At the Council the press played an essential role, serving as a sounding board of public opinion as the churchmen began to realize that a truly Catholic Church could not hide its doings from the world in which it played so important if inconvenient a part, and which it had the obligation to evangelize by preaching its Gospel to every creature.

While resentment at the unabashed inquisitiveness of the newshawks, radio and television reporters — not to mention the secular pundits and editorialists — was a continual experience of the prelates, the media people continued to obdurately ferret out even the most secret or sacred information from the interior of the Council itself and the machinations of both the conservative and progressive groupings.

There were plentiful leaks from the curia and the papal household as well as from the pensioni, colleges, religious houses and embassies where the conciliar participants were lodged. As the former cardinal of Chicago, John Cody remarked: "Any reporter worthy of his byline who coud not crack a Vatican secret after riding up and down in the Vatican's interior elevator, perusing the Italian press, reading between the lines in *L'Osservatore Romano* and crashing an embassy party or two should hand in his reporter's typewriter."

At the daily press briefings in the *sala stampa*, or Vatican press office, statements and opinions by the various speakers as reported by the clerical spokesmen who gave a summary of what had been said were questioned, analyzed and quarreled over by the newspeople in search of a story that would make a headline in their home organ.

Criticizing the tendency of the curial hierarchs to 'clericalize' the news and blame a bad press on the prejudices or enmity of the journalists rather than on the mistakes and misdeeds of the churchmen, Jacques Maritain had complained: "To many Christians, every acknowledgment of our deficiencies appears somehow as indecent. They appear to be afraid to give trouble to our apologetic."[2]

One achievement of the Council was the acknowledgement in the Pastoral Constitution, *Gaudium et Spes*, of the right of the laity to manifest their needs and desires with liberty and trust, and the obligation to make known their opinions on matters concerning the welfare of the Church (n. 37). Commenting on this development, the Dominican theologian, M.D. Chenu in a conference in Rome titled *VOX Populi, Vox Dei* (the Voice of the people, the Voice of God) asserted that public opinion in the Church had to be recognized as a "constitutional dimension." This fact was not, he said, a concession to liberalism in a democratic society. Rather it was the consequence of the nature of the Church as a community, the mystical body of Christ.[3]

Thus religious information was not to be considered the prerogative of the ecclesial authorities but a healthy experience of faith, an act of testimony amid the shocks of daily existence. The custodian of the faith was not to manipulate facts and information to fit them into a pattern of ecclesial government.

In a sense, this was seen as a belated tribute to the nineteenth century Cardinal John Henry Newman's contention in his famous sermon "On Consulting the Faithful" that had its roots in the early church's axioms, *Securus judicat orbis terrarum* (the whole of the earth [e.g. the faithful] gives secure judgment [of doctrine]); and in a fourth century test for orthodoxy, "that doctrine is authentic which is held *semper, ubique et ab omnibus* — everywhere, always and by all."

Popes John XXIII, Paul VI and John Paul I felt at home with the press despite the fact that their curial assistants frequently cautioned journalists against misrepresenting ecclesial happenings and religious developments. Then in 1971 Paul VI issued an instruction *Communio et Progressio*

[2]G. Zizola, *Restaurazione di papa Wojtyla* (Rome, 1985), p. 67.

[3]*Ibid.*, p. 66.

in which he laid down norms for the prosecution of the Church's aims by employing the mass media.

With the arrival of John Paul II, a master communicator with mesmeric qualities for impressing immense crowds took control of the See of Peter. In his very first gesture, addressing the overflow crowd in the piazza fronting St. Peter's Church and half the world on television and radio from the balcony of the papal basilica, instead of merely bestowing his blessing *Urbi et Orbi* — to the City and to the World — the Polish pope delivered a short discourse in Italian in which he promised his pontificate would prepare the Church and the World for the year 2000.

It did not take long to discover that the Pontiff, while determined to update the Church's involvement with the world, using every possible means of communication, intended to accomplish that apocalyptic mission for the millenium by reintroducing into the structure of the Church a line of development more in keeping with law and order in doctrine and discipline, than with the more or less free-wheeling charismatic evolution that followed the Council. One means of so doing was to manipulate the secular mass media.

The first sign of a new order of using the press was unveiled at the XII World Congress of the *Union Catholique de la Presse* in Rome in September 1980 when the mass media were lauded as an indispensable aid for projecting the historic mission of the Church into modern secular society. This turn-about from denouncing the press as a demoniac force, in the language of Gregory XVI, to a new and decisive change-over was engineered by John Paul.[4]

Pursing this policy, the new Holy Father had set out in the footsteps of his predecessor, Paul VI, to preach the good news of Christianity personally to all the world, criss-crossing nations and continents from his native Poland and Puebla in Mexico to Asia, Africa, the Americas and the Antilles.

Contrary to Pope Paul's visitations aimed at reconcilia-

[4]*Ibid.*, p. 69.

tion and carrying a peace-oriented message, John Paul's observations frequently stirred controversy from his limitation of "the option for the poor" at the 1979 Latin American bishops' caucus in Puebla, Mexico, by asserting "the rich also have souls," to his unbending moral admonitions to the American hierarchy in Chicago in October 1980. This had been preceded by his revelation to the French Church in Paris in May that year, that his pontificate would be a return to a disciplined pursuit of the Council's mandates.

Obviously favoring the conservative elements in the French church the pope was severely criticized by Andre Frossard, who deplored the pope's obvious downgrading of Jacques Maritain's "theology of terrestrial reality" that had formed the backbone of the Pastoral Constitution, *Gaudium et Spes.*

The observant Catholic, Jean Marie Domenach, deploring the circus atmosphere that accompanied many of the papal masses and appearances in football stadia and gymnasiums, said the pope was being used by the television magnates as a tool of the very consumerism John Paul was constantly denouncing.[5]

Opposition to the pope's policies was experienced on his visit to Holland, Germany, Switzerland, Brazil, and Nicaragua, to mention but the more obvious, when the pope met unconcealed hostility among many Catholics including nuns, clergy, and lay leaders. Not unconscious of this opposition, the Pope told journalists on a return from an overseas trip, "I do not think the eminent cardinals knew what kind of personality I am, and therefore what kind of papacy they would obtain."

Back in Rome, respected commentators feared that in entrusting the Vatican press office to a professional journalist but ardent *Opus Dei* member Joaquin Navarre Valls, with a cover in the American Archbishop John Foley as president of the Vatican's Communication Commission, the Holy See was playing into the hands of the very secularizing

[5]*Ibid.,* p. 71.

temptations the pope was condemning as hedonism, consumerism and avarice.

Despite its reputation as an arch-conservative spiritual movement, *Opus Dei* had some 70,000 members, most of them lay men and women of competence in the academic and business world and with substantial financial backing. Rumors in the Vatican persisted in claiming that the organization had supported the Solidarity movement in Poland and was willing to make up the Holy See's deficits as well as take over the so called Vatican bank. It had been severely critized by the majority of the Spanish bishops, the English Cardinal Hume and others for its over-bearing evangelizing methods and questionable financial manipulations.[6]

Meanwhile within the Church itself a series of confrontations erupted as a result of the Pope's determination to steer the further development of the Council's effects in directions he prescribed. In the matter of the selection of bishops a heavy papal hand became evident in dioceses that traditionally had the right to at least present candidates of their choice to Rome for consideration.

In Holland a whole hierarchy was imposed from above. In Paris, New York, and Boston, in Medellín, Colombia and Mexico City not to mention Italy and Poland, new cardinals were created of men known to be of a conservative cast of mind. Nevertheless a balance of forward looking as well as traditionalist prelates still seemed evident in the Church universal. The trouble, as one high prelate said, was that the pope was too obviously taking sides in disputes about doctrinal and disciplinary matters in various nations whereas in the past the pontiff had usually kept the peace among his quarreling sons, only preventing them from injuring one another.

Among the tasks confronting the postconciliar Church was the attempt made by the religious orders and congregations to update their rules and reappraise their way of life. This reassessment was in keeping the Council's decree auth-

[6]*Ibid.*, 115 ff.

orizing them to reconsider the manner in which they were spreading the Gospel and the tasks for which they had been founded, whether domestic or foreign missionary work, teaching the poor or the well-to-do, working with the impoverished and most abandoned, or praying for the church and the world in strictly cloistered convents or monasteries.

In their chapter of 1974 the Jesuits following the leadership of their Basque Father General, Pedro Arrupe, the black pope, so called from the color of the religious cassock he wore in contrast to the pope's white garb, had adopted the "option for the poor" as a principal endeavor for their missionary activities. This included a drastic change in objectives on the part of a large contingent in the society from the education of the scions of regal and wealthy families to a direct alignment with the poor in their hovels and slum areas, without however abandoning the universities and colleges they conducted in all parts of the world.

Said the ascetic Basque general, "alignment with the poor in their search for justice may alienate you from family and friends. If it requires you to go to jail, well, go to jail. I was in jail; and so was our founder Ignatius Loyola." This new direction requiring as it did a restructuring of the leadership and authority in the order displeased the Vatican.

Admonished by both Pope Paul VI and John Paul II for tolerating dissidents from papal policies within the Society, Father Arrupe was finally relieved of his position as the Society's general after suffering a stroke. Papal interference in the organization's internal affairs was greatly resented by a majority of its members and on the first ballot of their 1983 chapter or election assembly, they elected Father Peter Hans Kolvenbach, a Dutchman and orientalist, well acquainted with the Roman scene, who immediately proceeded to implement Arrupe's policies but in a less exposed fashion.[7]

Similarly, curial-inspired papal interferences with the election process of the Dominicans and Franciscans, a

[7]*Ibid.,* 103 ff.

harsh surveillance of U.S. congregations of sisters, interference with reorganization of the rule of some 8000 cloistered Carmelite nuns was greatly resented and caused the Master General of the male branch of Carmelites, Father Felipe Sainz de Baranda, among others, to utter rather strong criticism of Cardinal Jerome Hamer, prefect of the curial Congregation for Religious, as well as other over zealous curial officials.

Finally, the papal favoritism shown to the quasi-secret *Opus Dei* organization, giving it a bishop with juridical powers outside the control of local dioceses in which its members were working, and the partiality shown to other arch-conservative group movements caused considerable unease throughout the Church.[8]

Attacks on theologians and seminary professors due to the delations by overzealous colleagues and well-to-do Catholics organized in societies to protect the faith, were welcomed in Rome. However, the investigation of the pastoral practices of the American Bishops Raymond Hunthausen of Seattle and Walter Sullivan of Richmond, as well as the Zambian Archbishop Emmanuel Milingo and the cardinal of São Paulo, Everisto Arns, were not appreciated by the majority of their episcopal colleagues. They realized that they too could be the object of such inquisitional tactics as a result of delations by their critics and enemies.

Meanwhile, in churches throughout the globe, bishops were attempting to confront the problems of their flocks by seeking mutual assistance. Fellow bishops began meeting at regular intervals in Episcopal Conferences whose legitimacy was acknowledged by the Holy See but whose activities were looked upon with some disfavor by the Cardinal Prefect of the Congregation for the Doctrine of the Faith, Joseph Ratzinger. He challenged their right to teach as a collegial group maintaining that only the individual bishop in his diocese had a commission to preach the gospel.

Nevertheless, the bishops of the United States, of Canada, England and Wales, of South Africa and many of both

[8]*Ibid.,* 169 ff.

the Anglo and Francophone countries in Africa, India, Indonesia and the Pacific Islands, as well as gatherings of bishops on a regional or continental scale such as CELAM or the Conference of Latin American Episcopates and the Union of European Hierarchies, were meeting with regularity to confront the evils of moral and societal breakdowns and to curb the strife affecting their faithful and nations.

They were likewise promoting new methods of evangelization, liturgical adaptation and spiritual development that resulted from the continuing attempt to implement the decrees of Vatican Council II.

At the council a sharp debate had preceded the acceptance of the collegial principle. Members of the papal curia, led by the legists, Archbishop Dino Staffa and Pericle Felici, challenged the possibility of a twofold papal supremacy, *viz.* that of the pope acting on his own — *ex sese* — and that of the bishops with and under the pope teaching with uncontestable authority.

It was Archbishop Pietro Parente, then Secretary of the *ancien* Holy Office, who in the third session (September 26, 1964) broke through the dilemma insisting that the relationship between the pope and bishops need not conform to the logic of secular politics. Of its very nature, the relationship implied a mystery since it was dealing with spiritual matters and thus the realm of grace.[9]

He might have added that the phenomenon had a parallel in the quantum theory as applied to theology by Karl Rahner using terms such as complementarity or a symptotic convergence described by the renowned physicist, Nils Bohr.[10]

Parente's intervention undid the bloc preventing a positive vote on the matter, but it won him the taint of a traitor among his intransigent curial colleagues.

Implementing this conciliar teaching, Pope Paul VI had established the Roman Synod of Bishops calling for an

[9] X. Rynne, *The Third Session* (New York, 1966), pp. 49-50.

[10] J. Honner, "Unity in Difference," *Theological Studies* 46 (1985), pp. 480-482.

ordinary Synod every three years, and providing for special and extraordinary Synods at the pope's discretion.

In the preface to his *Motu proprio*, "Apostolic Solicitude," the pope wrote:

> "Observing attentively the signs of the times, we are making every effort to adapt the orientation and methods of the apostolate to the growing needs of our time and the evolution of society. Hence our apostolic solicitude calls upon us to consolidate by ever closer ties our union with the bishops "who the Holy Spirit has placed to rule the Church of God" (Acts 20, 28)... In these times of ours, so troubled and critical yet so open to the salutary call of grace, daily experience shows us how useful for our apostolic charge is this union with the bishops. We wish to do everything in our power to promote and develop this union in order "to have round us the comfort of your presence, the support of your counsel, the weight of your authority."[11]

In keeping with the pope's specification, these assemblies were to involve representatives of the episcopal conferences from around the globe as well as a percentage of papal appointees, and both Catholic lay observers and, at the pope's invitation, representatives of the non-Catholic churches and communions. A commission of fifteen prelates, 12 elected by the Synod, 3 appointed by the Pope were to prepare the agenda and oversee the implementation of successive synodal proposals.

While limiting the function of the Synod to an informative and consultative capacity, it was believed that as the synodal assemblies generated their own mechanism, they would gradually achieve the status of a deliberative body with and under the pope on the model of synodal rule in both the Orthodox and Oriental Catholic patriarchates. With extreme skill, the Roman curia had thus far managed to head off that development.

[11]Cf. G. MacEoin, *Synod '67*, pp. 189-190.

For the twentieth anniversary of the opening of Vatican Council II (Oct. 11, 1962) several Catholic journals and notably the *Tablet* of London had paused to take a reading of the effectiveness of the Council two decades later.[12]

Many Vatican observers considered the fact that in the 20 years since the Council, the Church had not achieved Pope John's main objectives, *viz.* world peace and the reunion of the Christian churches, as a great disfavor to contemporary civilization as well as to mankind. But many agreed that to consider this fact as proof that the Council was a failure was to totally misread history circumscribed as it was by the human condition or, theologically, by original sin. Down the ages, Councils had taken decades if not centuries before the full implications of their achievements were realized.

Actually Pope John had been warned by Cardinal Tardini in particular that councils in the past had inevitably caused great confusion if not chaos. While acknowledging this fact, John had nevertheless proceeded, convinced that only out of chaos — "unless the seed die in the ground" — would come a Church thoroughly renewed by the Spirit in a new Pentecost. Certainly the Council had buried the vestiges of the Tridentine Church and prepared the soil for the Church of tomorrow.

It was this achievement that seemed in need of reinforcement when suddenly there burst on the Church and the world Pope John Paul's announcement that he was summoning an extraordinary Synod of bishops to Rome in late November to celebrate the 20th anniversary of the Council's conclusion. Its aim was to attempt to recapture the unique *esprit* of communion that assembly had achieved.

[12] *Tablet*, 9 Oct. 1983, pp. 1004-1005.

2

Preparation

In the twenty years since the close of Vatican Council II, the Catholic Church has been involved in a time of troubles whose magnitude has not been equaled since the revolt of the sixteenth century Protestant Reformation. The result as much of the revolutionary character of the Council's constitutions and decrees, as of the disruptive world conditions surrounding it, the Church's current contretemps have worsened an ongoing split between hold-the-line Catholics and liberal-minded faithful intent on pursing the *aggiornamento* or updating of the Church called for by Pope John.

World War II unleashed a series of political, social and economic forces that led inexorably to the current global upsets from the clash between the capitalist and communist systems in the stand-off enmity between the United States and Soviet Russia, to a rash of disruptive nationalism in the prewar colonial states, and the rise of a fundamentalist fanaticism in Moslem-dominated lands.

To the threat of global destruction posed by the danger of nuclear war was added the nightmare of a possibly imminent collapse of the world's monetary system, the terrifying outbreak of terrorism on a global scale, the breakdown of moral values in the sexual and pornographic revolution and the drug anti-culture, as well as the debilitating effects of worldwide unemployment and hunger, the economic exploitation of the impoverished, and the risk of ideologically-inspired guerrilla warfare, not to mention a creeping atheism intent on destroying the fundamental idealism instinct in the human psyche.

Ironically in the Council's Pastoral Constitution on the Church in Today's World, a revolutionary attempt was made to accommodate the Church to the global situation surrounding it. This utopian endeavor brought into focus the internal split between traditionalist churchmen wedded to a concept of the world as the arena for the satanically inspired evils affecting mankind, and the more optimistic religious leaders who see the world as God's creation and therefore good and capable of salvation.

In bringing the Council to a successful close on December 8, 1965, Pope Paul VI and the 2500 Catholic bishops who formulated its decisions felt they had achieved the *balzo in avanti* — the leap ahead — prescribed by Pope John in his desire to bring unity to the Christian churches and peace to the world.

The Council gave new directions to many aspects of Catholic life. It sanctioned the use of local languages instead of Latin in the western Church. It encouraged active participation of the laity as readers, ministers of the Eucharist, and counsellors in the Liturgy. The Council did reaffirm "religious submission of mind and will" to both the pope's and the bishop's decisions. But it stressed the inviolability of the individual conscience and challenged Catholics to come to terms with the times in their political, social and economic endeavors. It also prescribed an ecumenical approach to Orthodox, Protestant, Jewish and other religions.

Critics of the Council pointed to the disruptive happenings in its wake. They deplored the exodus of priests, nuns, and brothers from rectories, convents and monasteries, many of them abandoning their religious calling to marry. They pointed to the frequently bizarre experiments with the liturgy and the challenge to catechetical instruction traceable to the Council. And they deplored the breakdown in sexual mores which they blamed on the Council's reordination of the primary purpose of marriage as love rather than the procreation of children.

More recently conservative Catholics had been encouraged by the hard line being pursued by the Vatican in dealing with apparently dissident theologians, priests, nuns, and religious orders not following the Roman curial line, and bishops thought to be lax in implementing papal policies. They pointed to the repressive actions of the German Cardinal Joseph Ratzinger who, as head of the *ancien* Holy Office (now the Congregation for the Doctrine of the Faith), had censored theologians, such as Hans Küng, Eduard Schillebeeckx, Jacques Pohier, and Leonardo Boff; his hypercritical evaluation of the doctrinal agreements between bishops and theologians of the Catholic and other Christian churches and communions, including the attack on his former professor, the eminent German theologian, Karl Rahner (recently deceased) for his optimistic appraisal of curent ecumenical achievements; his attempt to downgrade the teaching authority of national hierarchies of bishops; and his desire to emasculate the conciliar doctrine on the collegiality of the bishops with the pope in settling Church policy at the top.

They rejoiced likewise in Cardinal Jerome Hamer's harsh censoring of a group of US nuns who had the temerity to sign an advertisement in the New York Times stating that the Catholic teaching condemning abortion was not monolithic. They applauded recent papal interference in the internal affairs of religious orders beginning with the Jesuits and including the Dominicans, Franciscans and the Carmelite nuns.

Thus, the sudden announcement of his plan for a synod to a small group of cardinals in the Basilica of St. Paul's, Outside the Walls, after a prayer session for Christian unity, by Pope John Paul on Sunday, the 25th of January, 1985, that was fashioned to imitate Pope John's surprising announcement of Vatican Council II on January 25, 1959 and coincide with the twentieth anniversary of that Council's successful conclusion (December 8, 1965) came as a surprise, not to mention a shock, to Catholics and Vatican observers round the world. The pope said the two-week session (November 25 to December 8) would serve as an opportunity to relive the extraordinary atmosphere of ecclesial communion that characterized that assembly.

As with Pope John's original inspiration to hold the Council, the exact origin of John Paul's call to celebrate its twentieth anniversary may never be known. In each instance there seems to have been a spontaneous element — a grace or charism — that led to effects far beyond the original expectations. With the Council, John brought about a revolution in the Church's self-image and its attitude toward the world. With the Synod, John Paul took the measure of that turn-over and found it good.

Speculation about the Synod's agenda was split. One group felt it would enable the Pontiff to tighten control of Church teaching and discipline in keeping with the current rash of disciplinary warnings to theologians, church activists, priests and nuns who felt the Council enabled them to engage the world on its own terms. Others expected the Synod to give bishops an opportunity to inform the Pope and Curia of the actual problems confronting the Church in their respective lands.

Observers of papal policies were nonplussed by the short span allotted to preparation for the Synod and the rather vague papal agenda for its consideration. They felt the two-week assembly was too short a time in which to discuss important issues troubling the Church. They feared the Synod would prove a well-orchestrated, curial demonstration in which the heads of the world's Catholic hierarchies would be constrained to signify their support for John Paul's current law and order prescriptions.

Traditionalist Catholics were delighted. They hoped the Synod would give the conservative wing of the Church an opportunity to roll back many of the Council's actions. They wanted a return to the old-fashioned catechism in religious instruction, and a recall to the rectory and convent of priests and nuns now agitating for social justice in the streets.

Historically conscious Catholics were well aware of the conflicts that troubled the Church from the start. In his *Letter to the Galatians*, St. Paul admits having withstood

Peter to the face; and in the *Acts of the Apostles*, Luke describes the disagreement between Jewish and pagan converts over the service of widows and orphans as well as the problems raised by circumcision and dietary-laws.

Down the centuries following the practice of the provincial Roman consuls and military leaders who met at the conjunction of the great imperial roads (*syn* — together; *odos* — road) to interpret the Emperor's policies, such doctrinal and disciplinary conflicts were settled by gatherings of bishops in Synods and Councils seeking a concensus. To this day, synodal consensus is the rule in the Greek, Russian, and other Eastern churches. In the west, however, Rome gradually took charge of these assemblies, greatly diminishing their authority.

Current clashes in the Church are centered on an older view of that institution as concerned primarily with spiritual endeavors opposed to the Council's concept of the Church as wedded to the Modern world. In its constitutions and decrees, the Council embodied Pope John's prescriptions that the Church pay attention to the "signs of the times." Although promulgated by Pope Paul VI as sanctioned by the Holy Spirit, many of the Council's achievements were not welcomed by a large group of priests and laity.

They now felt that the moment of their justification had arrived. They wanted Pope John Paul to outline a positive, hard-line on all the Church's worldly commitments from its anti-abortion drive to a condemnation of homosexuality, birth control and sterilization. They wanted the bishops to be told to mind their own business in regard to national defense programs and to keep their hands off the economic and political problems of the nations. They wanted priests and nuns in religious garb confined to church, rectory, convent and cloister. And they wanted lay people out of the sanctuary.

Liberals, on the other hand, hoped the Synod would condemn the manufacture of nuclear weapons and the threat to use them as unquestionably evil. They wanted the Synod to censure the injustice of both communist and capitalist systems and condemn the international sale of arms as likewise absolutely evil. Finally, they wanted the Church to commit itself unconditionally to the "option for the poor" directing the full impact of its evangelizational efforts to uplifting the exploited and destitute around the world.

On opening the Council, John admitted that in the past the Church had frequently "condemned error with the greatest severity." Nowadays, he continued, "the spouse of Christ prefers to use the medicine of mercy." She believes in "demonstrating the validity of her teaching rather than in condemnations."[1]

In keeping with this specification, John Paul in a recent discourse called for a radical revision of the notion of progress and development to offset the "dehumanization and depersonalization" of modern society. Observers felt a similar request should be made of the Synod. The bishops should call for a radical revision of curial policies to encourage rather than restrain "the step forward in doctrinal penetration and the formation of consciences" that was John's design for the Council.

Such a prescription would require a considerable change in Vatican policy close to the top where recently a rash of repressive actions had shocked the Christian community and the outside world accustomed to hearing the pope insist on human dignity and human rights, freedom of conscience, and the right to practice one's religion freely.

Recent curial inquisitional tactics were seen as directly contradicting the Council's teaching on religious liberty, the inviolability of conscience, and a pluralism in doctrinal understanding that reflected the various schools of theology honored by the Church down the ages.

Apparently acknowledging such criticism, John Paul said that in these matters, the curial cardinals and particularly Cardinal Ratzinger spoke for themselves. He allowed his Secretary of State, Cardinal Agostino Casaroli, in a speech delivered in Brescia, the home of Pope Paul VI, to express a public though veiled criticism of the German cardinal's

[1]Cf. X. Rynne, *Letter from Vatican City*, Appendix I.

condemnation of the Vatican's dealing with communist countries.[2]

Meanwhile, sparked by a pessimistic interview given to the Italian journalist Vittorio Messori in *Jesus*, a conservative Italian periodical, by Cardinal Ratzinger and published in book form as a "Report on the Faith," last May, after the text was read and revised by the prelate, a running series of discussions, arguments and proposals for the Synod were given worldwide publicity.

In his interview, Ratzinger maintained that he honored Vatican II as an authentic ecclesial experience under the guidance of the Holy Spirit. However, he portrayed the post-conciliar period as largely a time of dissent, discouragement, decadence and self-destruction on the part of large groups of Catholics who, in their endeavor to put the Council into practice, were guilty of "every kind of heretical deviation." Asserting that the Council's documents got buried under an avalanche of immature interpretations (including, he might have added, a plethora of considerations by a youthful theologian named Joseph Ratzinger), he said a true understanding of the Council had not yet begun. Designating the current liturgical scene as "lopsided," he called for a "*restoration*" of the Church's doctrine and discipline in Scripture studies, seminary teaching, the liturgy, and a law and order reshuffling of the lives of priests, monks and nuns.[3]

In the post-conciliar period, Ratzinger had obviously undergone a radical conversion. A prominent young professor at the Council as a peritus or expert in the employ of Cardinal Joseph Frings of Cologne, he had early on joined the group of progressive theologians editing *Concilium*, a periodical dedicated to implementing the Council's existentialist conclusions.

In a talk to the Catholic Student's Association at the University of Münster soon after the Council, he had con-

[2]G. Zizola, *Restaurazione*, p. 217.

[3]*Ibid.*, p. 92-99; *Tablet*, 14 Sept. 1985, pp. 948-949.

demned the tendency of opponents of the Council to indulge a "pharisaical Qumranism" under the guise of fleeing from contact with the world as well as a refusal to accept any profane influence on the Church. By way of contrast, the Church, he said, did not intend to reconstruct its own little world for itself as it had tried to do when, under Popes Pius IX (1846-78) and X (1903-14) it repudiated all worldly values and thus destroyed its ability to serve as the '*Salt of the Earth*' and the '*Light of the World*'. Then suddenly, two years after the Council, he was discovered advocating the very attitude he had repudiated as "Qumranism."

Two elements seem to explain this turnabout. One was his attachment to the fourth century St. Augustine who in his conversion from Manicheism to Catholicism was unable to shake off a pessimistic attitude inherent in the heresy, not hesitating to label the vast majority of mankind ignorant of Christ as a *massa damnata* — damned to hell forever.

The other was his rivalry with his contemporary Swiss colleague, Hans Küng, whose books about the Council quickly became best sellers and whose students during the disruptive riots of 1968 frequently harassed Ratzinger causing him to abandon his professorship at Tübingen and retire to his native Bavaria. His departure was evidently traumatic, and he took refuge in a theology of traditionalism, joining the reactionary group organizing the periodical *Communio*.

This move recommended him to the conservative German bishops including Cardinal Joseph Höffner of Cologne and the Bavarian political community. Eventually, it landed him in the archbishopric of Munich and obtained for him a cardinal's hat before the death of Paul VI. Under John Paul II, he was called to Rome and made Prefect of the Congregation for the Doctrine of the Faith where, with the aid of Cardinal Höffner, he promptly persuaded the Holy Father to unseat Küng depriving him of his title as a Catholic theologian and forcing him out of the Catholic faculty at the university where he still lectures, however, in an ecumenical institute.

In league with the Dominican curial archbishop, Jerome

Hamer, like Ratzinger, a former apparently open-minded theologian, he inaugurated a minor reign of terror against non-conformist theologians, including one of his former students, the Brazilian Franciscan priest, Leonardo Boff, whom he accused of christological errors in his defense of Liberation Theology. Called to Rome, Boff was accompanied by two Brazilian cardinals, Aloisio Lorscheider of Fortaleza and Evaristo Arns of São Paulo.

Their gesture of support was a tactical mistake. Despite the fact that they had been early electors of John Paul II, they were given to understand that power pressure by outsiders did not work in the Vatican. Their man was condemned to a year of silence despite the fact that no shade of heresy was found in his writings. His primary fault had been his criticism of the curial government of the Church at the top.

A preliminary response to the German cardinal's "Report on the Faith" was issued by a group of Munich pastors, his former diocesan subjects, in the *Süddeutsche Zeitung* (*South German Times*, August 17-18). "Our pastoral practice has acquainted us," they asserted, "with the unhappy side effects of the conciliar renewal. However, we know that a Church that wants to turn back from Vatican II divorces itself from modern society and will be reduced to marginal significance. Those who, like Cardinal Ratzinger, exalt themselves in such a triumphalistic manner above everything that is not or does not seem to be Roman Catholic exclude themselves as partners in dialogue (with the world) ... Let the bishops in the Synod act as their predecessors did at the Council ... Confronting the current inquisition, let them work for freedom of thought, of conscience and of doctrine in our Church."

In their outburst, these churchmen refrained from asking the impertinent question as to why Ratzinger had spent such little time as archbishop of Munich. Might it have been in keeping with an old Roman adage, *promoveatur ut amoveatur*?

Almost in direct opposition to Ratzinger, the octogenarian cardinal of Vienna, Archbishop Franz Koenig, a principal actor at the Council and a primary supporter of Karol Wojtyla's candidacy at the Conclave allowed himself to be interviewed by the Italian journalist, Gianni Licheri, who published a running account of the cardinal's observations in a short monograph called *Dove vai Chiesa* — "Church, Where are you Going?"[4]

In a frank defense of the Council's achievements and its implementation over the last twenty years, the Austrian churchman insisted that without the Council, the Church would have fallen victim to a catastrophe. He described in detail the ferocious attempts of the curia, under the aegis of cardinals Ottaviani and Tardini, first to talk Pope John out of the idea of a Council; then to take control of both its preparation and activities.

Asked what he thought of Ratzinger's criticism of the Council's aftermath, he said it was obvious that the Prefect for the Congregation for the Faith was preoccupied with minor splinterings within the theological community.

Ratzinger had obviously obscured the authentic progress made by the Council in its recognition of the positive character of history, of science and the arts in the synthesis of human and divine interests leading mankind back to God.

Koenig said it was obvious that Ratzinger's fear of the prevalence of error and heresy in today's Church was not unlike that of his predecessor, Cardinal Ottaviani, who had been publicly repudiated by the first Roman Synod of Bishops under Pope Paul in 1967. He insisted that Pope John's repudiation of the "prophets of doom," in his inaugural speech at the Council, was still pertinent. What the Church should be doing, said the Austrian prelate, was not condemning theologians but presenting the world with a creditable answer to the enquiry, "Who is Jesus Christ?" that will be a pertinent concern of mankind to the end of time. In the final analysis, he was cetain that the mind-set of the Polish pope was not that of the German cardinal.

In late August, theologians of the Concilium group, apparently in answer to the Ratzinger interview, issued an open letter in which they contrasted the optimistic impact

[4]G. Licheri, *Chiesa dove vai?* (Rome, Borla, 1985).

on the Church of the Council and the pessimistic atmosphere they saw hanging over preparations for the Synod. Admitting that after twenty years the Council was seen as not free of certain imperfections and exaggerated optimism, even naivete, they nevertheless deplored the fact that "many of its positive initiatives were checked, distorted and even set at naught by the obstinate resistance of pockets of bureaucracy and other intemperate groups and individuals."

They asserted that it was not the Synod's function to help the bishops to look back twenty years; it was their obligation to assist them in looking forward to the year 2000. They concluded, "We ask them to speak out in a manner beholden to no one as is their right." Recalling Pope John's admonition at the start of the Council, they urged, "Do not listen to the prophets of doom who announce disasters as if the end of the world was at hand" . . . rather, they should repeat Christ's admonition, "Do not be afraid."

In similar fashion in a press conference, the cardinal of Belgium, Josef Suenens, one of the principal architects of the Council, insisted that the post-conciliar unrest was to a great extent conditioned by the reassessment which directly involved the world and not the Council as such. He insisted that with the passing of the years, the Council would be seen as a mighty breath of spiritual renewal. He agreed with Cardinal Lustiger of Paris who maintained, "The Council is not behind us; it is ahead of us."

Confronting the pessimists' hope that the Synod be a kind of '*restoration*,' a step backwards, a return to the past, Suenens said such a return to the *status quo ante* was inconceivable. "We must firmly reject the word '*return*'" he announced, "that would signify a rejection of the Council and delight both the acknowledged and secret ultra-conservatives."[5]

Two months before the Synod's opening, Professor Hans Küng, the controversial Swiss theologian, former colleague and rival of Cardinal Ratzinger, in a slashing diatribe

[5] *Tablet*, 12 Oct. 1985, pp. 1064-1064.

entitled "Speaking out after Silence" took both the cardinal and the pope to task, claiming: "What is happening to our Church in the eighties makes me both sad and angry, particularly after the conciliar awakening that made the sixties such hopeful years." Analyzing the German cardinal's stance, Küng ventured, "Joseph Ratzinger is afraid. Just like Dostoievsky's Grand Inquisitor, he fears nothing more than freedom..."[6]

Citing Ratzinger's record as Prefect of the *ancien* Holy Office, Küng accused him of personally passing sentence against the new French catechism at Notre Dame in Paris; condemning Karl Rahner's *Unity of the Churches: An Actual Possibility* (written with the German theologian Heinrich Fries) as theological acrobatics; of personally tabling the memorandum of the Anglo-Catholic International Commission on Reunion as premature; and attempting to correct the Latin American bishops in their option for liberation theology at Bogota.

In Küng's analysis of the cardinal's interview *A Report on the Faith*, Küng contended that "it boiled down in terms of practical politics to one thing: protecting the threatened power of Rome in which the *papacy* equals the *Church* equals *Christ* equals *God*" in an autocratic sense. Control over the souls of believers in dogma, morals and church discipline must, according to Ratzinger, be secured and reconsolidated by all possible means ... Once this curial power and its centrally directed Roman system were secured, the Church would be saved.

Turning his attention to the Holy Father, the irate theologian maintained, "These are not the mere contentions of an official of the Roman Curia ... they are symbols of Church policy of the first order; and in them one can hear the voice of the pope ..."

Küng continued by accusing Ratzinger of confessedly having difficulty in distinguishing between the morality of the Ten Commandments (as revealed to Moses) and the morality written in the hearts of created natures. "His pic-

[6]*Ibid.*

ture of moral theologians facing a choice between the Church's teachings and the world is a wild parody of the way they go about their business. To judge from his frequent references to the errors of "certain," "some" or even "many" theologians, the cardinal thinks his former profession to be in a woefully bad state.

Pointing to one source of the cardinal's pessimism, Küng asserts:

> It is frightening to learn that the cardinal thinks that the reports that cross his Roman desk every day give him a fair picture of what is going on in the life of the universal Church and in the work of theologians.
>
> Notoriously, some, even many, of the letters received by his office contain inaccurate and unjustified denunciations against bishops, theologians and others. That mail thrives on "horror" stories that the cardinal himself seems to relish...

In a typical Küngian peroration, he summed up the anticonciliar attitude of the papal court: "Instead of the programmatic language of the Council, we again have the language of an authoritarian teaching office; instead of an *aggiornamento* in the spirit of the Gospel, a revival of so-called traditional 'Catholic teaching'; instead of 'collegiality' of the pope and bishops, a revival of strict Roman centralism; instead of an opening to the modern world, renewed and increasing indictments, lamentations and denunciations."

Turning his attention directly to the Synod, the Tübingen theologian asserted: "The decisive question is, therefore, are things going to work out for the Curia this time as well? Are the bishops going to tell the truth? Are they going to address the tabooed needs and hopes of their congregations and clergy whether it be opportune or inopportune? Are they, where necessary, going to break the curial spell the way Cardinals Frings of Cologne and Liénart of Lille did at the start of Vatican II? These men protested the authoritarian procedure of that assembly on its first day, and thereby set in motion the unrestricted reflective action of the Council."

In conclusion, Küng reduced the bishops' actions to two possibilities. Either they would look for the future in the past and fall completely into line with the *restoration* course of the Roman curia; or they could plan the future in the present, and with Christian freedom, risk conflict with the curia just as the bishops did at Vatican II.

In ranging over the whole diapason of evils in the post-conciliar Church that he attributed to the papal bureaucracy, Küng indulged a slightly hysterical emotion particularly in his personal attack on his former colleague, Cardinal Ratzinger. In the minds of many observers, it took away the full force of the jeremiad.

Hans Küng's animadversions were in contrast with those of a Tübingen colleague, professor Walter Kasper, whose confidential paper on the synodal preparations written for the German hierarchy had received wide circulation and probably occasioned his appointment as the Synod's theologian.

Rejecting both Ratzinger's pessimism and the anguished cries of progressives who felt the Council was rejected by both pope and curia, Kasper said the distinction between a preconciliar and a post-conciliar Church was a mistaken concept even though the Council did introduce a new self-understanding of the Church. Among its benefits was the fact that "the sense of co-responsibility has been strengthened for both laity and clergy and put into practice, letting the Church experience itself as a true 'communion'." He insisted that more importance should be placed on the striving for holiness within the Church as its most important current need.[7]

Kasper concluded that it would be totally wrong for the Synod to utter a great cry of lamentation about the evils and the evidence of crisis in the Church. "If the Church continues along the lines laid down by the Holy Spirit at Vatican II," he said, "the conciliar ideal and reform of Catholicism will win through."

Last, but not least, the rebel Archbishop Marcel Lefebvre

[7] *Ibid.*

told journalists in his headquarters at Albano, outside Rome, that he took a less pessimistic view of the Church's current situation than did Cardinal Ratzinger. Nevertheless, he described the forthcoming Synod as "a great danger to the Church" and as the "second stage of a revolution that began with the Council and could lead to the Church's self-destruction." He hinted that "if in Rome there is a split with the tradition of the Church of old" he might ordain a bishop as his successor. This would then change his status from a disobedient bishop to one in schism — definitely separated from communion with Christ in the Church.

A man of considerable intelligence and extensive experience — he established the hierarchy in francophone Africa when archbishop of Dakar in the 1950s — he apparently sees his opposition to the progressive, conciliar evolution of the Church as providential, a position attested, in his estimation, by the fact that he has a large, well-educated, growing number of followers and 162 priests in his organization.[8]

Meanwhile in immediate preparation for the Synod, the episcopal hierarchies around the world had held conferences and consultations of their dioceses, faithful, priests and nuns, concentrating on the simplified questionnaire submitted to them by the Synodal Commission. They were asked how the Council was received in their jurisdictions; what was done to implement its decisions; what difficulties they had experienced; and how they were now engaged on its realization.

As a by-product of this preparation for the Synod, a number of national hierarchies expressed annoyance with recent Vatican actions. Many Latin American bishops, particularly in Brazil and Peru, were unhappy with Roman attempts to condemn Liberation Theology; the Spanish bishops resented the upgrading in ecclesiastical status of the conservative religious organization known as *Opus Dei* — the Work of God — over their protest; the Swiss bishops felt the recent decree legitimizing the so-called Tridentine Mass celebrated in Latin was a blow to their authority in favor of

[8]*Ibid.,* 16 Nov. 1985, p. 1215.

the rebel Archbishop Marcel Lefebvre; the Dutch bishops, though Rome's hand-picked conservatives, resented the close Vatican surveillance of their affairs; and the Italian episcopate, despite its proximity to the See of Peter, felt deprived of their prerogatives when the pope not only gave canonical recognition to the movement called Communion and Liberation, an archconservative, elitist group, against their advice, but removed from their episcopal conference the right to elect their own president, imposing the Vicar of his diocese of Rome, Cardinal Ugo Poletti, as their head.

In an extremely frank evaluation of the Synod's preparations, speaking for the English and Welsh bishops, Cardinal Basil Hume of Westminster decried a lack "of tolerance and a new fundamentalism" in the Church. He said the Synod's effectiveness would be limited by the brevity of its duration — 55 working hours by his calculation.[9].

The US hierarchy in their report to Rome insisted that American Catholics were "fundamentally on the right path" in carrying out the Council's directives despite the view of some critics (viz. Catholics for the Faith and such newspapers as the *Wanderer*).

Observing, however, that "fewer people have studied the Council's documents than speak of them; and fewer still have made it their own than have studied them," they stressed the actuality of the collegial process achieved among the bishops themselves, and in the cooperation of their priests, nuns and lay apostles. Citing recent teachings of their Conference regarding local and worldwide justice along with personal morality in social situations, they insisted that "listening, dialogue, and consultation" were now taken for granted in their teaching process as was evident from their recent Pastoral Letter on War and Peace, and the letters they were preparing on the Economy, the Laity and the place of women in the Church.

The Dutch hierarchy, like the British and the US bishops, had published their animadversions of the coming Synod and the Irish and Swiss were about to do likewise when an

[9]*Ibid.*, 14 Sept. 1985, p. 953.

admonition arrived from Rome forbidding further such publications. Caught in a bind, the Irish bishops launched a presynodal Pastoral Letter that called for "a less complacent attitude" towards the world's ills, and less "preoccupation with the institutional features" of the Church. Seemingly, they thus placed themselves in line with their European colleagues.[10]

On a slightly different tack, Bishop Jean Vilnet of Lille, speaking for the French hierarchy, advised that after take-off, a satellite often needs correction to keep it in its proper orbit. Hence, he felt, the Synod would perform a useful service for the Council.

An optimistic estimate of the Synod's possibilities was delivered by Bishop James Malone of Youngstown, Ohio, President of the US Bishops Conference, at their annual meeting in November. He said collegiality would definitely be a primary concern of the Synod. In contrast to Cardinal Ratzinger's disapproval, Malone felt the pope was seeking closer collaboration with the bishops in responding to the needs of particular churches round the world. He indicated that the Synod would strengthen the ecumenical movement and reaffirm in a positive fashion the Church's option for the poor in its outreach for peace and social justice.

To the immense satisfaction of the American hierarchy, the Vatican's pro-Nuncio in Washington, Archbishop Pio Laghi, supported Bishop Malone's contention. He praised the collegial fashion in which the US bishops had produced their Pastoral Letter on Nuclear Warfare and lauded their current efforts to produce a significant Pastoral on the Economy.[11]

While Vatican watchers looked for sinister motives behind a consistorial assembly of the College of Cardinals called by John Paul to meet three days before the Synod, the nuncio's strong pitch in favor of what he termed an effective working collegiality seemed a more reliable indication of the way the wind would blow in the Vatican during John Paul's Extraordinary Roman Synod of Bishops.

[10] *Ibid.*, 12 Oct. 1985, pp. 1075-1076.

[11] *Origins*, 15 (1985) pp. 388-392.

3

The Implementation (I)

Three weeks before the opening of John Paul's Extraordinary Synod, an editorial on the Papal Ministry appeared in the authoritative Jesuit bi-monthly, *Civiltà Cattolica*, whose contents are perused before publication by experts in the Vatican's Office for Public Affairs. The import of this long, sinuous argument was the fact that in substantiating papal primacy and supremacy, as defined by Vatican Council I, Vatican Council II had changed the framework of the teaching.[1]

Vatican Council II, while in no way derogating from the pope's supreme and immediate power over the entire church, had modified that attitude substantially. The third chapter of the Council's Dogmatic Constitution, *Lumen Gentium*, in outlining the Church's hierarchical rule, described the papacy as a service and not a domination. It stressed the collegial concomitants of the papal office in keeping with Christ's injunction to Peter, "and you once fortified, strengthen your brother," as well as the command, "Feed my lambs and feed my sheep."

The editorial cited the fact that in consequence of the aura of transcendence and sovereignty that had become so prevalent after Vatican Council I, a so-called *infallibilism* had

[1]*Civiltà Cattolica*, 2 Nov. 1985, pp. 209-221; cf. F. Murphy, "The Politique of the Synod," *America* 153 (1986) pp. 49-51.

arisen — a concept totally opposed to the idea of infallibility. It expressed an integralist mentality that confounded infallibility with impeccability and extended the Petrine gift beyond the truths of revelation.

Infallibilism, the article continued, is a psycho-social attitude, not infrequently attached to servility, typical of a courtier mentality that underlies the pyramidal conception of the Church, and leads to aberrations of papolatry and courtly Byzantinism.

"To us it seems that for the present crisis, solutions should be discovered that are inspired by pure Gospel doctrine ... The papacy should reveal itself as the humble servant of the unique Saviour ... as the unpretentious servant of the human conscience, rejecting the human temptation to both despotism and paternalism."

The editorial asserted that curial centralization of power at the apex of the Church gave too much influence to the Roman bureaucracy with its unceasing effort to achieve uniformity of belief, liturgy and discipline at all costs. Hence, the editorialist deplored the loss to the Church of the riches of other cultures and the authentic development of a pluralism in doctrinal explanation and mystical experience.

The burden of the *Civiltà Cattolica* editorial was contained in its final paragraph where the editor insisted: "for those who live in communion with Christ in the Church — this was a significant change from the prevailing, sixteenth century, Bellarminian insistence on allegiance to the Roman pontiff — it will be a demonstration of faith and joy to live in faithful obedience to his vicar ... and when one realizes he must dissent 'in word or gesture' he will act with the interior and external respect which sons are accustomed to use in discussions with their father."[2] This Civiltà article, with its no-holds-barred critique of papal decisiveness and curial dominance, seemed to indicate the Pontiff's awareness of recent criticism of the pope's hard-nosed policies and the growing fears that the synodal assembly would prove to be a

[2] *Civiltà*, p. 221.

smoke screen behind which the Vatican bureaucrats would dictate its results.

Observers of the editorial asked at once whether its publication, obviously sanctioned by the Vatican, meant that the pope was actually rethinking his role as supreme pastor and might possibly take the advisement of counsellors from outside Rome to mitigate the harsh judgments of priests, nuns, theologians and bishops emanating from the curial offices. While there was no immediate confirmation of such a radical change, there were signs that some minor mutations were in the air.

One was the list of twenty cardinals selected by the pope for participation in the Synod in which his choice seemed to balance off the conservative American Cardinals, Law of Boston and Krol of Philadelphia, the Brazilian, Eugenio de Sales of Rio de Janeiro, Jean Marie Lustiger of Paris, and Archbishop Jerzy Stroba of Poland with the more progressive cardinals, Aloisio Lorscheider of Brazil, Anastasio Ballestrero of Turin, Angel Suquia Goicoechea of Madrid and Richard Vidal of Cebu in the Philippines.

Of considerable significance, likewise, was the pope's homily at the Mass in St. Peter's on Sunday opening the Synod. Confining himself almost solely to the doctrinal and pastoral significance of the Feast of Christ the King, the Pontiff had warmly welcomed all the participants in the Synod — cardinals and bishops, representatives of the Laity and the non-Catholic observers, requesting their full cooperation in the work of the assembly.[3]

Three days before the opening of the Synod, the Holy Father convoked a consistory of the world's cardinals referring to it as an introduction to the Synod. Commentators were concerned lest it was called to set a pattern for the synodal development and thus destroy that assembly's credibility even before it got started. No such danger emerged.

[3]The sermons, speeches, interventions and summaries were published in *L'Osservatore Romano* (English ed.) 9, 16, & 23-30, Dec., '85, and in the Holy See's Press Office each day during the Synod.

Instead the pope had called them together to discuss the reform of the curia, the papal bureaucracy that had been on the agenda since Pope Paul's attempt to restructure this governative organ in 1967 when he introduced a change of nomenclature, but failed to remove the old-guard cardinals and prelates from their offices, thus preventing any real reform.

His most obvious failure was discernible in the *ancien* Supreme Congregation of the Holy Office and the Inquisition whose name he changed to the Congregation for the Doctrine of the Faith and whose function he described as encouraging the development of theological research and doctrinal application. By failing to retire the septuagenarian pro-prefect, Cardinal Alfredo Ottaviani, *l'enfant terrible* of the Council, the inquisitional habits of the older organization prevailed only to be reinstated with vengeance by the current incumbent, Cardinal Joseph Ratzinger.

In introducing his current attempt to redimension the curia, John Paul praised the loyalty and competence of this body of officials and denied that there was a dichotomy of understanding or policy between the Holy Father and his associates. John Paul asserted: "The primacy of the Pope as successor to St. Peter calls for unity with him through obedience. Some false ideas tried to set up a kind of opposition between the bishops, the curia, the Synod, and the pope as though the curia was a 'parallel power' or a kind of sieve, to filter the activity of the pope. Diversity of opinion in the church can help, but it can never involve isolationist or centrifugal tendencies." Nevertheless, this body was in need of updating.

Among the measures to achieve this end, the pope had taken advice from the presidents of the Episcopal Conferences who should know best the snags in relations between the Vatican and the residential bishops; but, thus far, no definitive solution to the problem had been discovered.

In response, a number of cardinals spoke with some vigor beating back attempts to downgrade the Secretariat for Unity and its cognate secretariats for non-Christians and for non-believers. The move to make them mere commissions or councils under the control of the Congregation for the Faith would certainly be looked upon as a step backward in the ecumenical movement.

The desire likewise to strip the Secretariat of State of its political appearances was rejected as juvenile. As Cardinal Casaroli, the Secretary said, "This office by whatever name would have to confront the world in which the Church was operating on political terms, and its Office for Public Affairs would have to function as just that."

In the end, the pope chose to table the matter and attention was turned to the papal financial situation with a possible 50 million dollar deficit in 1986 staring the pope in the face. Much of the expenses came from updating the salaries and benefits of the Vatican's 3000 employees now mostly unionized, as well as inflation, and the expenses connected with the pope's international travel. Nothing was said about the scandals surrounding the Institute for the Works of Religion, popularly known as the Vatican Bank, whose financial dealings were involved in the collapse of the Ambrosian Bank of Milan, a former Catholic bastion of financial stability, the matter having been dismissed from the Italian judicial calendar.

The Synod's first session convened on Monday with Cardinal John Krol's address of welcome. He was acting as one of the three presidents of the assembly with Cardinals Jan Willebrands of the Curia and Joseph Malula of Kinshasha, Zaire. Their task was to arrange the speaking order, see to the proper alignment of the Synod's business and keep the speakers to their eight-minute limit.

Krol quoted the Holy Father as totally wedded to the concept of the Synod as an "instrument of collegiality and a strong expression of communion ... in the service of the local churches and their mutual communion." "The pope," he continued, "did not summon us to celebrate a mini-council of our own, or to change or correct Vatican Council II. Rather he wants us to relive the ecclesial communion that was the Council, exchange experiences on how we implemented its decrees and seek new ways of applying the Council to the needs of the Church and the world today."

Describing the concept of communion, Krol quoted an ecclesiastic who in the 1969 Synod contended, "This is not just a communication of external goods. It is an internal participation of the persons themselves. In this way, the collegiality of the bishops corresponds to the nature of the Church." The bishop was, of course, Karol Wojtyla, the present pope.

Striking a personal note, the cardinal of Philadelphia suggested that in confronting today's world, the bishops should implement the new Code of Canon Law which, as a renowned canon lawyer himself, he maintained formed a triangle with the Word of God in the Scriptures and the documents of the Vatican Council. He, thus, atributed to the law a substantial rather than a regulative role in the Church's structure — a concept not totally shared by Pope John who on being told by an ancient-of-days Dominican professor of law that the regulations produced by John's 1960 Synod of the diocese of Rome were not law, but exhortations, replied: "They may not be law in your book, but they are in mine. And I'm the pope."

Round the pope some 160 prelates were gathered in the new Hall of Audiences, begun by Pope John and completed by Paul VI, enabling 10,000 people to have an unrestricted view of the Holy Father in the main chamber and a spacious expanse for precisely such gatherings as the Synod in what used to be called the "hall of broken heads" from discarded statuary relegated in the old building.

Attending the Synod were 106 elected presidents of their national and regional bishops conferences — cardinals, archbishops, bishops — some twenty-one appointees of the Holy Father, twenty-four members of the Roman curia, three Superior General of Religious orders — Jesuits, Salesians and Benedictines — ten especially invited Orthodox and Protestant observers, plus a handful of the laity, including Mother Teresa and the clerical resource people (*periti*), simultaneous translators and press briefing officers.

In a benevolent gesture, the Holy Father had invited to the Synod a group of retired cardinals and prelates who had played prominent roles at the Council and allowed them to speak of their experiences at moments of pause in the Synodal activities. They included Siri of Genoa and Suenens of Belgium, Koenig of Vienna and Volk of Germany, Marty of Paris and Munoz Vega of Ecuador, each of whom took advantage of the opportunity at pauses in the discussions to address the assembly.

By the pope's special request, the retired cardinal, Gabriel Garrone of Toulouse and the curia, initiated this series with a resume of the *esprit* and atmosphere of the Council in order that the synodal fathers, two-thirds of whom had not been at the Council, might savor its elan. This he did with a neat gallic brevity. Garrone attributed the perspective opened by the Council that enabled it to rediscover the Church in the full light of the faith and in view of a dialogue with the world, provided the conciliar assembly with surprises that were all spiritual experiences. They included different aspects of the Church, its nature and mission by which the visage of the Church was illumined with new clarifications.

> It was an extraordinary experience, but an experience of a unique council. John XXIII had committed the bishops to a path not yet marked out. It was not, as in the past, a matter of responding to a precise problem of the faith, but, as he himself had said on the very day of the solemn opening, a matter of the "adherence of everyone, in a love renewed in peace and serenity, to the whole Christian doctrine in its fullness. . ." The Pope left to the members of the Council the task of choosing the way to translate into operative terms the general mission that he had indicated: that of presenting to the world Christ's message in a true and authentic dialogue. Once the manner of formulating the work was decided upon, the Council never departed from it: the one object was to be the *Church* in herself and in her relationship with the world. This simple and integral perspective was to unify all of the conciliar work: to offer to future dialogue with the world the true countenance of the Church in which it is found.

The actual business was begun by Cardinal Godfried Danneels of Belgium, as the Synod's special Secretary General, with a *relatio* or resumé of the responses to the questionnaire sent to the 106 Conferences of Bishops round the world. Some eighty percent had responded, several admitting their inability to gather the necessary information on time, and one, the Bishop of Gabon, confessing that although the Vatican documents were never delivered by the local post, he and his colleagues responded to information they obtained from the newspapers.

Danneel's summation was brief and to the point. Remarking that the twenty years separating the Synod from the Council were the space of a generation, he felt they were sufficient to provide a vast panorama for the Council's evaluation. It offered a propitious moment to stop and reflect on the changes, the emerging realities, and new needs to which the council's teachings should be adapted. Summarizing the Synod's objective as an attempt to recapture the ecumenical spirit of the Council "through a participation in the sufferings and the joys, the struggles and the hopes that pertain to the Body of Christ in various regions of the world," he described the work of the special Secretariat as a seeking out the mind of the local churches.

Acknowledging the fact that there was no *instrumentum laboris* or working paper to guide the synodal discussion, he said that with the aid of the Synod's theologian, Professor Walter Kasper, he had divided the material received from the various hierarchies into four sections, beginning with the relationship between the Vatican Council and the current Synod. The Synod was to deepen the Council's achievement and in no way to reverse it. Next, he had listed both the positive and negative elements in the bishop's reports. Citing the gains in sacramental consciousness brought about by the liturgical renewal, the current attention being paid to the Scriptures at all levels of Christian living, the role of the laity in all features of the Church's life, the positive approaches to ecumenism with the Church's voice raised loudly and courageously in support of human rights, peace and freedom, he said it was obvious that the post-conciliar Church was alive, and living with intensity.

Listing the negative aspects of the post-conciliar experience, he said the relationship between the Church and the world was so much more difficult now than it had been 20 years ago. Asking how current problems were to be solved, he aserted that "post-conciliar deficiencies could not be dealt with by preconciliar remedies." Reminding his audience that after each Council in the past there had been grave tensions and disturbances, he said this was a sign of life calling for a rediscovery of the Church's true nature, which was a *koinonia* or a mystical communion reaching out to all of mankind.

In a press conference that same day, the Belgian cardinal replied to a question as to the role of Cardinal Ratzinger in the Synod, asserting that the assembly was not called to discuss a book; nor was it to provide an arena for a boxing match. Asked about the conflict between curial use of papal authority and the role of the Bishops Conferences, he replied: "This question of the two-fold authority of the pope and of the college of bishops has been with the Catholic Church since the time of Peter and Paul and the apostles. And I do not think it will be settled before Jesus Christ returns."

The actual interventions began on Tuesday morning with the cardinal of Lima, Peru, the tall, jovial Franciscan, who privately admits a fascination with New York City and the Franciscan monastery on East 31st Street. He asserted:

> "The Council was a new Pentecost. It aided the Church to know itself better and to address the world more decisively. It forced us to pay attention to history; and particularly in Latin America to listen to the poor, thus gaining credibility by highlighting the collegial nature of the episcopate and the essential role of the laity. Now we must question those seeking security by believing that everything possible has already been done, or thinking that everything remains to be done. A proper Christian atti-

tude is based on faith, which provides us with the grace of conversion and renewal."

Cardinal Stephen Kim of Seoul, Korea, agreed that the Council meant the onset of both a new ecclesial self-understanding and a spiritual renewal of the Church as a communion aimed at the salvation of all mankind. Kim made the point that as a western event, the Council had to be seen as a passage and a transition in the Orient. It demanded time and a deliberate pace to have its decisions translated into so many diverse cultures to be met with in the Asiatic continent. Thus, the need for stabilization, while acute, must not stifle this living process through narrow interpretations of the conciliar documents.

Next taking the microphone, the Ukranian cardinal Myroslav Lubachivsky, residing in Rome, asked the synodal fathers to keep in mind the "cruel realities" of religious persecution in the Soviet Union where there are still some four and a half million Catholics forced into the Orthodox Church. While the bloody persecutions of the post-war period have ceased, the blatant denial of religious freedom is stronger than ever. This fact cannot be ignored "in diplomatic silence."

For Ukranian Catholics living in Russia, the second Vatican Council never occurred, since no Catholic bishop, priest or lay person is allowed to function religiously.

Admitting that the Ukrainian Church in union with Rome was an obstacle to ecumenical relations with the Orthodox partriarchate of Moscow, the cardinal still repeated a frequent request that his Church be given the status of a patriarchate that would provide his now hopelessly scattered flock (with about one and a half million in the United States, large groups in Canada, France, Germany and other parts of the world) with a truly visible and authoritative rallying point, thus preserving the rite. This the Vatican has strenuously opposed on jurisdiction and ecumenical grounds.

Archbishop Denis Hurley of Durban, South Africa; a

leader in the anti-apartheid movement, presented the results of the consultation of the South African bishops conference. In regard to internal church relations, he said, the principle of subsidiarity should operate in the sharing of responsibility between the Holy See and the local churches as well as in the mutual cooperation between Conferences of Bishops and other bishops grouping on a regional or continental level. He saw no danger of lessening papal supremacy in this ecclesial structure if each entity kept in mind that the Church was a communion in and around Christ, with the bishops as successors of the apostles grouped around Christ's vicar in collegial fashion and commissioned to go out, "two by two" to preach the Gospel.

In the matter of internal evangelization of the faithful, Archbishop Hurley said the Conference stressed the need to communicate the "splendid theology of the Gospel" and the magnificent Council documents as well as Pope Paul's great Encyclical *Evangelii Nuntiandi* on *Announcing the Gospel* (of 1974).

Finally, he asserted that the Synod should be concerned with the requirements of practical evangelization rather than theology. "Prophetic statements are relatively easy to make," he concluded, "It is living them out that is extremely difficult. Hence, we should concentrate on this obligation."

The Ukrainian archbishop of Winnipeg, Canada, Maxim Hermaniuk, next said that to implement the collegial government of the Church as proposed in *Lumen Gentium*, the Dogmatic constitution with whose first two chapters he was intimately involved at the Council, a permanent Synod of Bishops composed of electees by the current Synod with appointees by the Holy Father, should be erected with legislative powers under the Pope to decide with his authority all the questions in the life of the church that are today decided by the Holy Father with the Roman curia. This would reduce that bureaucratic body to its proper exercise as an executive and not a policy setting instrument. It would likewise be in keeping with the patriarchal structures of the early Church where consensus rule prevailed.

The archbishop had made similar proposals in preceding Synods only to find his suggestions unsupported by his fellow bishops and ignored by Rome.

The archbishop of Poznan, Jerzy Stroba, next addressed the gathering saying that the principal reason for the crisis of secularization confronting the Church was the crisis of European culture that profoundly affected the reception of the Council's teaching with the secular press often leading to the spread of misinformation. In confronting the skepticism affecting so many of the youth today, theologians should be furthering the study of the concept of the Church as the "people of God" thus giving to the new generation of Christians an intimate function in spreading God's word.

The first speaker to broach the topic of inculturation was the archbishop of Tamana, Ghana, Peter Poreku Dery, who, he asserted, had been present at all four sessions of the Council as a bishop.

Quoting from the consultation of the Conference of Bishops of Ghana, he said that as a result of the Council, the Church in Ghana had become more ecumenical and more mission and missionary-minded. They felt that the Holy See should put more trust in the bishops of a local Church in implementing the mind of the conciliar documents. In particular, Rome should leave enough scope to these churches to sustain the process of inculturation and allow them to grow to full maturity by taking on their own cultural identity in matters of life and worship.

The true vision of the Council maintains that salvation concerns the whole human person in all its dimensions and has given impetus to the socio-economic commitment of the Church. It thus has an important evangelizing significance. Hence, the necessity of a renewed and active participation of the laity. As a result of a Pan-African Laity Seminar in 1971, there was no need to convince African Catholics that the Church is for all and not peculiarly for the clergy. In entrusting the laity with confronting the enormous evangelization, economic, political and social difficulties of today, we should not be in too much of a hurry. Above all else, the Synod must recognize the role and ministry of women in the

Church. After all, they constitute more than half of the faithful.

One of the first synodal fathers to witness to the endemic nature of the *comunidades de base*, the small basic Christian groups pursuing their social and economic uplift based on a community absorption of the Gospel, was Bishop Jean Margeot of Mauritius. He said the Council had brought to his island new and fundamental intuitions that were renewing the Church in a radical fashion.

The first of these intuitions was the concept of the Church as a mystery of communion between all its members. The second regarded its mission in service to the world. The latter was being purused in a very human manner by the ecclesial base communities.

In these small gatherings, by way of the catechesis of adult Christians, the faithful are rediscovering the Word of God that is leading them to a personal adhesion to Christ. Through these communities the poor become the evangelizers and artisans of the Kingdom of God; and priests rediscover the people of God in a pastoral service that stimulates their creativity along with a profound conversion.

Next, approaching the microphone, Cardinal Richard Vidal of Cebu in the Philippines, said that with 43 million Catholics, two-thirds of whom are of Asiatic stock, the Church was fully involved in the affairs of the world. In the wake of the Council, the need to distinguish sociological from ecclesial involvement was necessary so that priests do not deprive the laity of their rightful function in the religio-political order. At present, the Philippine Church is being conditioned to the local culture, and is striving to achieve justice and toleration for all its people.

Cardinal Paul Poupard, curial Secretary for the Secretariat for non-believers, spoke of the immense task incumbent upon the Secretariat in contacting and organizing a dialogue with a practical and ideological atheism so prevalent in today's world. Designating atheism as a wound in the heart of modern culture, the cardinal outlined several successful encounters with non-believers, such as the Science and Faith discussions at Ljublana in Jugoslavia, and colloquia between members of Episcopal Conferences and university centers of recent vintage.

Bishop John Gran, the retired bishop of Oslo, stressed the essential function of the collegial process in Conferences of Bishops particularly in lands where the Church was so minimally represented (as in Scandanavia). Asserting that the mechanism of the Synod had not thus far achieved the effects hoped for by the Council, due to Roman interference (eg, the necessity of submitting documents and statements to Rome for surveillance before publication), he said the principle of subsidiarity should be put into practice more effectively. This meant that matters of both doctrine and discipline should be handled on levels where they originated in the Church and only referred to higher authority when no proper local solution could be found.

A principal reason for this demand is that bishops are administrators of the Word in their own right as successors to the apostles. They are not representatives of the Bishop of Rome. Thus, he felt that the Synods had not yet reached their potential in assisting the Bishop of Rome in ruling the universal Church.

The cardinal of Cologne, Joseph Höffner, asserting that the liturgical revolution was well accepted in Germany, pointed to the moments of crisis that had disturbed the faith of many in the wake of attacks on tradition and the stability of both Church and civil governmental bodies in the late 1960s and 1970s. In particular, he pointed to a loss of faith among the youth; the fact that many Catholics were now picking and choosing what they would believe. To offset these evils, the cardinal said the Gospel was not to be interpreted in sociological terms. Rather a new attention must be turned to unity in the Church, rallyng around the Holy Father.

Cardinal Anthony Peter Koraiche, the Maronite patriarch spoke next. Citing the catastrophic political and military happenings in the Near East that seemed to "forecast the end of the Oriental Christian Church in those lands," the patriarch insisted that the Christians of the eastern rites were not second class citizens in the Church or merely splendid archaeological survivals as Rome seemed to treat them. They witness explicitly to the traditions of the primitive churches and have given witness down the ages to the charism of martyrdom, that is also a current experience as the cross is being gradually eliminated from Islamic lands.

Bishop Francis X. Hadisumarta of Malang, Indonesia asserted that instead of insisting continually on the centralized exercise of authority, the Roman curia should encourage the local churches to develop the Spirit of the Council in full responsibility in taking up the challenge of the Gospel presented by the Asiatic peoples in the path of their modern development. He called for suggestions from the Synod on how to interpret the code of canon law in reference to marriage, laicization, the liturgy and the development of a contestual theology, the selection of bishops, and the Church's opening to the people of diverse religions and social cultures in the Far East.

Biship Ivo Lorscheiter of Santa Maria, Brazil said the fruits of the Council have been largely positive in Brazil in the liturgical and biblical fields, in a renewed missionary spirit, ecumenical action, social work, the option for the poor, and the development of new structures within the Church. Divisions do exist. They manifest themselves in superficialities or radicalizations that dishearten the faithful. The Council must be seen as a light, not a limitation. Subsidiarity and the principle of collegiality need further study and implementation. Catholics should avoid making unjust accusations within the Church as well as against people of other churches and religious traditions.

Bishop Gregory Singkai of Bougainville and the Pacific Islands testified to the fact that due to a national self-study based on the Council, the churches of Papua, New Guinea and the Solomon Islands are alive and enthusiastic in their inner being and work, despite difficulties ranging from the need to get religious instruction into the government schools to a better confrontation between clergy, laity and hierarchy by way of mutual inspiration.

Bishop Anselm T. Sanon of Burkina Faso and Niger, in Africa, said that by the end of Vatican II the church in (former) Upper Volta-Niger had been functioning for 65 years. In 1977, welcoming a fundamental option for the Church family, the churches had turned their attention to the task of accommodating local religious beliefs to the Christian creed beginning with belief in the Trinity. For the first time, he said, the Word of God began to resound in our own languages.

In order to remain open to their human virtues, the Church must promote other peoples' human and cultural progress. The union of the Gospel with western culture has made its mark. Now it is time to evaluate the mentality of new people coming into the Church. Our option for the Church-family implies communion in which lay people and priests are co-responsible for the evangelization in which ancient and new churches work together in a collegial union and fraternity to induce the inculturation of the faith and the emergence of a theology and history of African expression.

The archbishop of Salzburg, Karl Berg, suggested that collegiality must be the expression of a *koinonia* or mystical communion between the world's bishops and the pope, leaving centralism and particularism as lesser values. The coresponsibility of the laity must be taken seriously. Ecumenism in Austria is a working activity through the orgnization known as *Pro Oriente.*

As regards increasing marriage problems, the need for a matrimonial catechumenate is obvious. In addition, the Church must take to heart the problem of the distancing from the sacraments of the divorced and remarried in order that through the way of mercy, after sincere repentance, they might be readmitted to the sacraments. It is likewise necessary to reflect further on the problem of responsible parenthood faced with advances in medicine; and the concept of nature must be more deeply studied.

Completing the second day's interventions, the archbishop of Tokyo, Peter Seiichi Shirayanaggi, made a similar plea for the reinstatement in the Church of the divorced and remarried. He mentioned the fact that Catholics were so few in Japan that mixed marriages were inevitable and that after mistakes, there was little chance of a man or woman remaining unmarried. Hence, he called for a more merciful approach to this problem for his suffering people.

These two interventions in favor of giving the sacraments to divorced and remarried Catholics who had not obtained an ecclesial annulment caused considerable stir in the press. In particular, Bishop Berg's reference to procreation and his remark concerning further study of "nature" were considered a challenge to Rome's intransigency in following the dictates of Pope Paul's encyclical *Humanae Vitae.* The archbishop was asked to clarify his meaning by several members of the press. In so doing, he managed to avoid the issue; and it was not pursued by the synodal fathers.

One immediate result of the Synod was the emerging realization by the participants that the Church's center of gravity had shifted substantially from the Europe-North American axis to the so-called Third World of Asia, Africa and Latin America. While Western Europe, North America, Australia and New Zealand had but 28 presidents of Episcopal Conferences, and communist Europe 10, there were 76 presidents from the three continents of the currently underprivileged world: 26 from Africa, 26 from Latin America and 24 from Asia and Oceania. It was this circumstance that made the discussion of inculturation so crucial a concern of the Synod. The subject was put into proper perspective by Bishop Georges Singha in a written intervention that set the style for the position taken by a number of the African hierarchies.

Africa and Europe are united by particular historical ties. The first to enter the Church was Europe, which marks it still with her tradition and culture. Would it, therefore, be mistaken to say that our present Church, that we call universal, is in large part traditionally and culturaly European? The word "culture" especially regards all peoples, all continents, and thus the Universal Church as well. The Universal Church is a reality already, but it is not yet totally present, because not all the cultures of the nations of the earth are represented in the Universal Church.

The life of the Church is also the history of the meeting of the various peoples of our planet. This is true for the future as well. How the Church builds her history, becomes aware of it, and draws the consequences is of capital importance for the witness that she must give to the world, our world, in which meetings are often transformed into conflicts. The problem of the meeting of peoples is also that of the meeting of cultures. This brings us to the question of unity, which is not a synonym of uniformity, nor of standardization, nor of levelling, but which must go hand-in-hand with diversity, differences, variety and perhaps multipliticty.

Vatican II did not shelter us from problems. Let us face with courage those that present themselves to us, so that the work of the Council will be completed.

Bishop Gabriel Zubeir Wako, Archbishop of Khartoum, Sudan, following this line of concern, informed the gathering:

> The local hierarchy in Sudan is ten years old. They have been ten difficult years for the local bishops, who had to rebuild a Church devastated by civil war and utterly weakened following the mass expulsion of the missionaries from the country. After the first years of groping with no older hand to guide them, the bishops drew up a National Pastoral Plan whose main objectives were, "A well programmed Spiritual Renewal at all levels and a sustained program of on-going formation for all pastoral workers." This set the Church in Sudan on the paths of Vatican II. At times the bishops felt they were abandoned, and that often made them ask: "Where does a Church like ours feature within the Universal Church?"[4]

Vatican II very much stressed the doctrine of communion, unity and collegiality. The universal Church must, therefore, see herself as a communion of all the local and particular Churches united with and under the leadership of the Bishop of Rome. This vision requires that there be real

[4]*Tablet*, 7 Dec. 1985, p. 1299.

collaboration, cooperation and mutual concern for one another among the local churches.

The problems of growth, inculturation and self-reliance that many young local Churches face should be the concerns of the Universal Church — the concerns of the whole body. The young Churches need encouragement and accompaniment in their efforts to tackle these problems.

If the Church is to grow organically, she should pay special attention to the local Churches that show signs of weakness. She should adapt her pace, evaluate her structures, and adopt a language that fosters communion, unity, and collegiality and that gives even the slowest and weakest local Church the sense of belonging. The implementation of the decrees of Vatican II needs the speculation of theologians and other scholars, but should not stop there. To make the council a living reality, we need men and women who are committed to accept the challenge and the pain of real conversion. Without conversion of heart, no change is possible in the Church.

Giving witness to the grave problems affecting his Church, the archbishop of Chad, Charles Vandame, said:

> The Church of Chad is the last born among the African Churches. She has experienced grave trials: cultural revolution, war, famine, and thirst. She has known the difficulties of the post-conciliar period. In spite of this, she continues to grow.
>
> The exercise of collegiality at the level of the Episcopal Conference of Chad is very fruitful. But it is not enough. There is a need to promote instances of collaboration which are much richer at both the regional and continental level.
>
> A great problem in Chad is the organization of ministries. It is not in conformity with *Lumen Gentium* and the decree on the priesthood — *Presbyterorum Ordinis*. Actually, the local Christian communities are so numerous and scattered about that the priest is no longer a member. He come from outside. He passes through

> rarely and rapidly. The faithful organize themselves without him. This poses a dual problem: a) some ordained ministries are here assumed by the laity; b) communities come together on the Lord's day without the Eucharist.
>
> The burst of vocations will not be capable of remedying this situation. The institution of the permanent diaconate would permit the resolution of the first problem. But we hesitate to proceed along this path. By resorting to the "priesthood of married leaders," of these communities, it would be possible to resolve the second problem, but new difficulties would be introduced.
>
> The bishops of Chad do not see clearly what the best solution would be. But they point out this problem: the majority of the Christian communities live without the Sunday Eucharist and without hope that this might change.

The bishop of Franceville, Gabon, Felicien Makouake, admitted that the Bishops Conference obtained information on the Synod from the newspapers and not the post. Nevertheless, he said:

> The fruits already obtained from the Council are numerous: Sacred Scriptue is better known, the Liturgy better understood and more active through the introduction of the songs, rhythms and gestures meaningful to the sensibility of our people; there is an effort towards inculturation, especially in catechesis where the redaction of a national catechism is underway; a more fraternal Church, more responsible laity, spiritual renewal, especially after the visit of the Holy Father (1982).
>
> Many difficulties remain: the small number of "apostolic artisans," the absence of large seminaries and other institutes of formation, the dangerous evolution of society, the race for money, power, pleasure; spiritual insecurity, fetishism, and sects. But hopes remain: in spite of the recent competition of Islam, the Gabonese are very open to the Christian faith.

He expressed a final wish: that the Synod might help the church to defend the heritage of the Council and that the young Churches might be encouraged in their effort towards the evangelization of human cultures.

Similar observations were made by the bishops of Lome in Togo, the archbishop of Cotenou in Benin, the cardinal of Kampala, Uganda, and the bishop of Gweru in Zimbabwe speaking for their individual hierarchies.

An interesting intervention was made by Bishop Adolfo Herrera of Camaguey in Cuba who, on thanking the Lord for the Council, expressed particular gratitude to the Council for not having condemned anyone. He said the Cuban Church had obviously not been on the mind of the fathers at the Council; and it was now tied to a particular socio-political experience not provided for by that assembly. Following Pope John's suggestion, the Church has learned that the serene proclamation of the Gospel and the joyous exercise of faith has more power than any condemnations or defensive attitudes. The Cuban Church is now preparing for a five year ecclesial reflection at the national level that will consist of a review of our Church in the light of the Gospel, the council, Medellin and Puebla.

In his intervention, Archbishop Marc McGrath of Panama suggested that the subjects now being aired at the Synod might be reconsidered after a two or three year interval. And Bishop Bernard Hubert of St. Jean-Longueuil, Canada caused a minor stir when he moved that the present Synod be adjourned and a second session be held in two or three years time. This would, he said, give the prelates time to study the profound issues they were facing in so short a period. He likewise asked that the Synod prepare its own Message for the Faithful instead of leaving it up to a curial committee as had happened after the last few Synods.

Almost in response to this request, the Irish Cardinal Thomas O'Fiaich said the first and central message of the Synod must be "to proclaim loudly, humbly and in unambiguous language its adherence to the decisions and doctrines of the second Vatican Council"; and secondly, to promote the "careful and prayerful study of...the Constitutions, Decrees and Declarations which make up the rich legacy of that Council to the Church."

The use of vernacular in the Mass had improved immensely the quality of participation by the laity (a survey in his own country had shown that 87 percent of all Catholics attended Mass weekly and 30 percent at least twice a week). But he observed that, compared with the reverence, alertness and enthusiasm he encountered whenever he celebrated Mass in one of the African countries, "the Sunday congregation in many European countries including my own seems tired and indifferent. I'm afraid that the only place where an Irishman sings enthusiastically is in the pub."

Further advances in the involvement of the laity were necessary. Half the population of Ireland was under 25 years of age and some young people found it difficult to identify with their local church: "We need to create local parish communities in which young people will have a sense of belonging and where their personal contribution to the parish community will be encouraged and appreciated. And we need to ensure that all church bodies of laity have equal representation from women and from men, so that instead of becoming alienated as in some countries, our women will have ample opportunity to use their gifts of compassion and warmth and friendliness in the service of the Church."

Cardinal O'Fiaich said that the Church must be "unrelenting in its pursuit of justice. We must leave no one in any doubt that the Church is on the side of the poor, the oppressed, the marginalised — not only in words, but also in deeds." Finally, he said that, coming from a part of the world where religious discrimination and sectarianism still survived, he could not praise "highly enough" the work of the Secretariat for Christian Unity during the past quarter of a century. Lest its high standing among Protestants should be affected by any changes in its rank, he was happy to support the proposal (already made by previous speakers) that it should be raised to the status of a congregation in the Roman curia.

In one of his written interventions, the cardinal of Rio de Janeiro, Eugenio de Sales, had addressed himself to the relations between bishops of dioceses and the religious monks and nuns working in a diocese. By law most of these orders and congregations enjoyed exemption from the bishop's control in the internal life of their convents and monasteries. Not infrequently difficulties arose about the manner in which they conducted their pastoral or educational activities and the bishop's policies. In his written submission the cardinal said:

The decline of religious life is one of the gravest ills of the Church. In many cases, its form of life — relaxed and influenced by worldly trends and secularism — causes grave harm to the universal and local Church.

It seems that major superiors often do not govern effectively.

The matter of exemption must be reviewed, because it is not justified except to the extent that it means a greater willingness and a more generous obedience to the Pope.

There are excellent religious. But there are many who have weakened respect for the Pope and who directly or indirectly oppose the Roman Curia. As regards the Conferences of religious: there must exist only those of the major superiors, not of religious in general. Major superiors must not easily delegate to the conferences their sacred duties as those first responsible for the formation of religious life and of each religious.

The authority of the bishops is not only juridical, but also involves a true spiritual responsibility for religious life in his diocese.

By a strange coincidence, the superior General of the Society of Jesus, Father Peter Hans Kolvenbach in his written intervention delivered what could only be considered a deliberate response to de Sales' attack that could only have been perpetrated after de Sales obtained the nod from Cardinal Jerome Hamer, the Prefect of the Congregation for Religious and not inconceivably of even higher authority in the Church.

The Jesuit General began by citing the Council's insistence on the communion that must always exist among members of the People of God "in such a way that the single parts of the Church collaborate by the common sharing of all things and by the common effort to attain to fulness in unity."

This ecclesial communion must exist in a particular way among the bishops, successors to the Apostles and pastors of the Church and Religious, who "tending to sanctity by the narrower way, stimulate their brethren by their example."

In order to promote this communion and to overcome more easily the difficulties that present themselves, the Congregations for the Bishops and for Religious, directly interested in these problems, published a document in May 1978 regarding the Mutual Relations between the bishops and religious in the Church.

It is necessary that general principles be kept in mind in order to promote the greatest collaboration between bishops and religious in the common task of the evangelization of the world.

The experience of these twenty years following the Council shows that it is opportune to develop the following principles:

The diversity of the hierarchical and charismatic gifts must remain the theological foundation of the *mutua relatio* or mutual relationship of bishops and religious. The one Spirit of the one Lord for the edification of the one Church is at the origin of these gifts. The multiple practical questions that arise find answers not so much in new directives as in an open dialogue listening to the Spirit who is the source of these gifts.

The tensions desired by the Spirit of the Lord for the good of the Church between the hierarchical gifts and the charismatic gifts should never constitute a factor of division or favor a parallel apostolate, but should lead to the dynamic enrichment of sanctity and apostolic zeal in the Church. It is a question then of respecting not only the internal autonomy of religious families, but also the specific missions that derive from their charisms.

In the summation of the four days of oral and written interventions, as an *instrumentum laboris* for discussion in the small language groups, Cardinal Danneels and his theologian, Walter Kasper, seized upon the notion of mystery as a key factor in describing the Church and its activities. Under this heading, they located mankind as the object of the realm of spirituality in relation to Christ and the Church.

From this viewpoint they branched out to discuss the pastoral consequences, the Word of God, and the Church as communion, respecting the pluriform dispersion of the local churches in their cultural trappings. In this perspective, the collegiality of the bishops in local and national hierarchies as well as in their direct involvement with the See of Peter became comprehensible and without danger to papal supremacy, always a curial worry.

Both the ecumenical dialogue and the relation between bishops and theologians came in for concern as did the significance of *aggiornamento* in its ecclesial connotation and in focusing the Church's attention on the modern world.

On Saturday morning, the prelates separated in their respective language groups: two French, two Spanish, two English, two Italian, and one German and one Latin. To his surprise, Cardinal Hume discovered that in the twenty-four English speaking prelates in his group, he was the only European.

During the Synod sessions, the pope sat in silence, occasionally jotting down what seemed to be a note or two. Actually he received an enormous number of prelates and people in private audiences; had small groups of bishops, non-Catholic observers and others in for lunch or dinner and went silently about his daily chores, receiving delegations from organizations visiting Rome, delivering short sermons on occasion, and enjoying contact with priests, laity, and prelates from round the world.

4

The Parallel Synod

That all roads lead to Rome was amply illustrated by two synodal phenomena. One was the gathering of cardinals and prelates — devout men from every nation under the sun —of all colors, political structures, and religious rites for Pope John Paul's Extraordinary Synod of Bishops.

The other was a superfluity of journalists and media people, likewise of world-wide provenance, who had evidently convinced their editors and producers back home that the Synod would be a newsworthy event.

As several commentators observed, what amounted to a parallel Synod was constituted by the press briefings and conferences in which journalists reflecting the interests of the Church and religion more generally, attempted with searching questions and inquisitive observations to penetrate into the more provocative arguments being aired in the synodal discussions. Early on, a prime topic was the influence of Cardinal Ratzinger's pessimistic evaluation of the state of contemporary Catholic theology on the assembly. Put to Cardinal Danneels as a question in his inaugural press conference, the answer was none.

The danger that the Synod would prove to be a 180 degree reversal of the Council and the Church's updating was likewise tossed aside by the English briefing officer, Fr. Diarmuid Martin and the cardinals and prelates who participated in a number of press conferences in the Vatican *sala stampa* and the USO facilities where the American Cardinals Dearden and Law with Archbishop May of St. Louis and Malone of Youngstown, Ohio, submitted to a batch of inquiries with full television coverage.

Microphones of cassette players and TV cameras were everywhere one turned in the vicinity of St. Peter's, particularly in the Press Hall and the Piazza of the Holy Office fronting the Synodal Hall of Audiences for the arrival and departure of the cardinals and prelates including the pope and curial officials.

With the unanimous denial by the interviewed that there was any question of "restoration" despite requests for greater surveillance of doctrine and discipline by a small coterie of overconcerned prelates, the attention of the journalists was turned on the problem of Liberation Theology in Latin America and inculturation in Asia and Africa. Here they ferreted out the clash between the so-called Lopez Trujillo faction (the feisty cardinal of Medelliin in Colombia, who as former president of CELAM—the Latin American Bishops Conference—rallied the "anti-option for the poor" prelates at Puebla in 1979 apparently with the Pope's acquiescence) and the Dom Helder Camara group including the two Brazilian cardinals, Aloisio Lorscheider of Fortaleza and Evaristo Arns of São Paulo with the cardinal of Lima, Peru, Juan Landazari Ricketts.

Questions regarding the possible reversal of the Council were likewise dismissed as irrelevant by Cardinal Joseph Malula of Zaire, Archbishop Henry D'Souza of Calcutta, president of the Asiatic Bishops Conference, and Bishop Dario Castrillon Hoyos of Pereira, Colombia, in a press conference on November 30th. Both Malula and D'Souza made it clear that a synopsis of the interventions of the first few days would serve as a position paper for the round of discussions in the small language groups that were to follow.[1]

Under question from several members of the press, cardinal Malula said the scope of the Synod was not to furnish

[1]Cf. *Il Tempo*, 1 Dec. '85, p. 23.

answers for specific problems troubling the Church. It was to shine the light of Christ's teaching on the life of men and women today, aiding them to regain a true, interior, spiritual dimension in their lives after experiencing the fact that material possessions and well-being were not a safe or sure way to happiness and spiritual fulfillment.

To a barrage of questions regarding liberation theology in Latin America, Bishop Castrillon indulged a "tempestuous attack" on the movement. Asked whether he agreed with Bishop Ivo Lorscheider, secretary general of CELAM, who was a strong supporter of this theology, Castrillon said he did not, if the bishop was "trying to justify or legitimize all the strands in liberation theology which have led to disorder and errors." (We can never bless hatred or violence. I do not recognize a Church that sets such goals as a Church of Christ.)

He then launched out on a denunciation of the so-called "popular Church" which, he said, pretended to be with the poor, but was not. It had compromised itself with trade unions and political parties and turned the Mass into a political meeting.

He distinguished, he said, "between a Church dedicated to help the poor, that lived with the poor, that itself experienced poverty and denounced injustices everywhere" and a Church that ... "accepted violence in contrast to the Gospel and that attempted to estrange itself from the magisterium of the Church, the authority of the Pope and the local bishop". He said he certainly did not recognize Christ in a Church with a machine gun. Warming to his topic, he gave as an example a scene in which a popular Church group requested to have the Blessed Sacrament exposed on the altar during a political rally, and when refused by the local prelate, tried to take the monstrance from his hands. Asked where this happened, he replied with vehemence, "In Nicaragua!"

A contribution to this debate had been furnished by the cardinal of Mexico, Arripio Ahumada, a bystander at the Synod, who circulated a letter printed in the Spanish edition of the *L'Osservatore Romano* (Dec 1) that declared "in the name of a group of cardinals of Latin America," that the Church in Latin America was going through a time of great difficulties, especially as concerns the integrity of its faith. The letter pledged "total adhesion to the magisterium of Your Holiness" and expressed gratitude to the Congregation for the Doctrine of the Faith for its 'rejection of the errors of a certain theology of liberation which, with the so-called popular Church, has caused so much harm to the faithful'.[2]

In the Synod itself that position was enunciated by Archbishop Raul Primatesta of Cordoba, Argentina, who criticized the popular Church as "leaning towards Marxist positions and attacking the hierarchical structure as if they were of human invention."

In several written communications to the Synod, the cardinal of Rio de Janeiro, Eugenio de Sales, constituting himself as one Italian journalist wrote, the advocate of an ecclesial "police state", denounced "grave dogmatic and moral errors" taught in "seminaries and theological schools". There were professors "who teach their own doctrines and opinions and not the doctrine of the Church". He recommended "apostolic visitations" which should have practical consequences.[3]

An obvious attempt was made particularly by Cardinal Lorscheider and his cousin, Bishop Ivo Lorscheider in written submissions to counter the influence of Cardinals Höffner and de Sales on this question.[4]

Ivo Lorscheider supported the principle of subsidiarity while admitting the difficulty of reinstituting the practice within the historical context of Roman centralization that had developed over the past few centuries. He suggested the gradual implementation of this practice by means of

[2]*Ibid.*; *Tablet*, 7 Dec. '85, p. 1296.

[3]*La Repubblica*, 3 Dec. '85, p. 7.

[4]E. J. Dionne, *New York Times*, 4 Dec. '85; *Tablet*, 7 Dec. '85, p. 1295; *La Repubblica*, 3 Dec. '85, p. 7.

encounters between the bishops and the Holy See such as the present Synod.

In some manner, he wrote, the Synod should contest preconceptions that are unfavorable to the initiatives of the local churches. They are trying to express the Christian faith according to their legitimate local customs.

In defense of liberation theology he insisted that it was a legitimate reflection of a spontaneous charismatic happening, whereby the poor under the inspiration of the Gospel were gradually achieving a fundamental human dignity in the social and economic world through an authentic spiritual experience. This theology was not the result of theory based on European theological movements. Nor was it in any way violence oriented, or Marxist inspired. It was the result of an orthodox Christian experience.

Cardinal Lorscheider supported these contentions, submitting interventions on the nature of the Church as a communion that strengthened the collegial aspect of the Bishops Conferences on local, regional and continental levels without in any way impinging on papal supremacy or on the independence of a bishop in his own diocese, a concern that seemed to be a principal worry of the Roman curia. It was a specific assistance to ecumenism and the development of a mystical communion peculiar to Latin America.

He further contended that the Church today as the people of God demands a new attitude on the part of the magisterium, viz., that it humbly listen to the poor; that it modify itself, letting itself be questioned on the message of the Gospel with Christ's own preference for the poor.

Basic to the dispute over liberation theology was a 1984 Vatican document published under the authority of Cardinal Ratzinger of the *ancien* Holy Office that stated: "The theology of liberation proposed a novel interpretation of both the content of the faith and of Christian existence which seriously departs from the faith of the Church and in fact constitutes a practical negation" (thereof) (VI, 9).

Refuting this charge, the Uruguayan Jesuit theologian, Jon Sobrino, not only rejected its contention, but demonstrated that the basis of this misrepresentation was a clear misreading of Vatican II's teaching. It renewed the dualism that had been rejected in the Pastoral Constitution, *Gaudium et Spes.*

The Vatican officials had introduced a two world theory separating the spiritual from the material world as if the latter were evil and the work of the devil. This led them to separate the religious from the secular, the Church from the world.[5]

As a result of petitions from a large number of Latin American bishops including the group of ten Brazilians who had written an open letter to the Holy See in support of Fr. Leonardo Boff, deploring his silencing as unjust, the Congregation for the Faith promised that a new declaration would be published taking into account the representations of the bishops. Under pressure from Cardinal Lorscheider, this new document was promised for February or March.

During the second day of the intervention, the metropolitan archbishops of the Malenkar and Malabar rites of Keraka in South India — respectively, Archbishops Anthony Padiyara and Joseph Powathil — who claimed a history of their churches going back to foundation by St. Thomas the Apostle, complained bitterly of the lack of respect for the integrity of their rites by both the Roman curia and the Latin bishops despite the Council's absolute insistence in its Decree on the Oriental Churches on respect for the integrity of their ancient rites and their customs.

In his intervention, Archbishop Padiyara asserted, "In our churches the exercise of our fundamental rights in the pastoral care of thousands of our people who have migrated to the large and small cities of India are impeded." This is due to the rigid insistence of the Latin hierarchy on the principle, "One geographical territory, one ecclesial jurisdiction." This is contrary to the Church's teaching.

He was followed by Archbishop Powathil who enlarged on the notion of communion and pluralism in the Church before complaining of the limitation of the Malabar rite's

[5]*Church and the Poor* (London, SCM, 1985); cf. *Tablet*, 29 June 1985, pp, 680-681.

evangelization efforts outside Kerala by local Latin bishops who do not want to deal with another church penetrating into their territory.

The problem seemed confined to the Indian situation for in both Europe and the Americas there were a profusion of Oriental rite churches in all the major Latin rite dioceses who enjoyed independence with full cooperation of the local Latin ordinary and the bishops of the various Oriental jurisdictions.

To the surprise of the synodal fathers, Archbishop Henry D'Souza, secretary of the Asian Bishops Conference, rose to refute the Keralan bishops' contentions by stating that in a missionary situation individual rites should not attempt to force their culture on new Christians, but allow the church to grow out of the local situation.

The suggestion appeared strange to most of the prelates for in preaching the Gospel and introducing a liturgical life, the missionary had no choice but to introduce his own customs, eventually allowing local traditions and customs to be blended in.

This matter was further pursued in an interview given to Ms. Cokie Roberts of U.S. National Public Radio and published in *La Repubblica* by the diminutive but outspoken Bishop Francis X. Hadisumarta of Malang, Indonesia, who complained that the Roman curia paid little attention to the bishops from his part of the world.[6]

On another tack, he acknowledged that there were moral problems in whose solution the churches in the Far East did not see eye to eye with Rome.

On the question of contraception, he said, we are most concerned about marital relations, particularly because of the economic conditions in which our people live. Hence, we are content to tell people faced with impossible situations that the use of such means must not disturb their conscience. We have been called to Rome on the issue when Cardinal Hamer was still Secretary of the Congregation for the Doctrine of the Faith. We have not said that the use of contra-

[6] *La Repubblica*, 8 Dec. 1985, p. 6.

ceptives is licit, but that it is up to the individual's conscience. Asked if he thought the Pope would change the rule, he said sadly, "No. Never."

Turning to the immediate tasks of the Synod, he said, the Church had to allow the evangelization of the Far Eastern peoples to follow their nature and cultural development.

In following the almost universal demand for inculturation, theologians pointed to the practice of the primitive churches. Once the primitive heralds of the Gospel scattered to the four corners of the Mediterranean world, the Gospel mysteries were interpreted in keeping with the mind-set of the people being evangelized. In Alexandria, for example, greatest stress was placed on the divinity of Christ in keeping with the Platonic philosophy there prevalent; in Antioch, it was the humanity of Christ that received fullest attention based on the Aristotelian approach to reality. And in Rome, a preoccupation with law and order resulted in a legalistic interpretation of Christ's moral teaching, and the evolution of the Primacy of the Roman See.

In a press conference on December 2, conducted by Cardinal Jan Willebrands, Cardinal Paul Zoungrana of Ouagadougou in Upper Volta, and Bishop James M. Hayes of Halifax, Canada, the Dutch cardinal and president of the Vatican's Secretariat for Christian Unity, put emphasis on the significance of the Synod for the ecumenical movement.[7]

Pointing to the presence of the ten representatives of the non-Catholic churches at the Synod, Cardinal Willebrands said they were given all the privileges of the delegates except a vote. They listened to the interventions and speeches and sat in on the small language circles.

In response to a journalist's question, Willebrands insisted that there had not been a recession in the ecumenical movement as was being whispered here and there in the Church. The dialogue was not only between bishops and theologians of the various churches, it had entered into the daily life of the Church as was evidenced by the visits of

[7] *Il Tempo*, 3 Dec. 1985, p. 21.

Popes Paul and John Paul to the World Council of Churches' headquarters in Geneva and the cooperation of the faithful in prayer meetings, social action and mutual understanding all over the globe.

Questioned about the possible entrance of the Catholic Church into the World Council, he said it was agreed on all sides that the move would be premature. Despite mutual cooperation at all levels, the Catholic Church was still too formidable an institution for current membership; it would intimidate some of the participants.

On the problem of inter-communion in the churches, he said the theological implications were profound and not yet fully clarified. All the churches agreed that without total doctrinal agreement no true union could be achieved.

In response to a question about liberation theology, the cardinal reacted somewhat testily. Criticizing those elements in the movement that put too much emphasis on the social and economic aspects, he said, these interests were essential, but did not represent the heart of the matter. "For the Christian, true liberation denotes his interior liberty, his spiritual liberty." He thus seemed to miss a main point behind the reality that for the millions of the impoverished, living in degradation, hunger and want, there is no possibility of exercising the interior liberty necessary to achieve true human or spiritual dignity.

Cardinal Zoungrana emphasized the fact that the Council had been an inspiring revolution for the African churches, freeing them of European domination by insisting that its faithful were the "people of God" and therefore God's family and not merely an offshoot of the Roman Church.

Zoungrana was joined by Archbishop Hayes in asserting that the Pope's voyages to their countries had been beneficial, breaking down barriers of custom and language, as well as prejudice and giving an example of the true universality of the Church to all their people.

Meanwhile, in both the secular and religious press, specific topics from the problems of divorce and remarriage, to birth control and laicization, and from a married priesthood to the ordination of women and clericalization, touched upon in individual Synodal interventions, but not gone into by the Synod, were pursued with some vigor.

Among the pundits furnishing in depth analyses of the issues underlying the synodal debate, were two editorialists on *Il Tempo*, Augusto del Noce and Gian Franco Svidercoschi. Claiming that the Synod had unearthed a series of new considerations for the Church, Svidercoschi said the disruptive forces that had troubled the Church in the developed world with crises in doctrine and discipline after the Council, had not greatly affected the new churches in Asia and Africa. This indicated that the secularized past and the new industrialized societies cannot be the measure for judging the challenges confronting the Church in these worlds.[8]

In Latin America where the Council has definitely had a fundamental effect, there has emerged an unavoidable obligation of pursuing the liberation of men and women from the exploitation of industrialization and the monopolistic international corporations.

In Africa, the anthropological problem with all its consequences on the plane of inculturation had to be faced with spiritual forces endemic to those societies.

And in Asia, the great debate with the non-Christian religions and the need to live in the reality of extremely deformed situations called for a new type of evangel.

These are the situations that must now be analyzed in their totality and not given partial answers from the fount of curial wisdom. They must be faced with a deep and sustained pursuit of the wisdom embodied in the Council's documents that are still far from being fully understood.

Augusto del Noce began by asserting that the Church is in need of a new epistemology or rationale of Pastoral theology in relation to its disciplines of doctrine and morals. He praised the effort made by the Council to comprehend the nature of the world as it actually is — *wie es eigentlich gewesen ist* — before applying the norms of belief or morality. This has always been the theory which has been neglected by the tendency in recent centuries to apply the

[8] *Il Tempo*, 3 Dec. 1985, p. 21.

Gospel norms and natural law indiscriminately to situations only partly understood.[9]

Now the world has become so complicated and the analysis of behavior situations so difficult, that the great temptation is to abandon the rational pursuit of criteria from reason and revelation, and to take refuge in *integralism* where certainty reigns. But this is the sin of escapism and has led to the horrors of contemporary ideological and political movements.

After analyzing the roots of the rise of fascism and the attraction of communism, with its zeal for justice, and its promise of utopia, del Noce tackles the notion of "restoration" and by sleight-of-hand logic, claims that the traditionalist is the true progressive, while the innovator is bound to repeat the mistakes of the past.

Archbishop Loris Capovila, Pope John XXIII's one-time secretary, in *Il Tempo*, asked how people would have extricated themselves from the network of snares and problems of the second half of this century without the great event of the Council. Certainly, he said, the road from the Council to the present has not been a freeway, but more like a caravan route, compelling voyagers to adapt themselves to the irregularities of the terrain. But risks are written into the logic of works and progress as Pope John maintained in starting the Council.[10]

In an interview with Archbishop Marc McGrath of Panama, *Il Tempo* quoted the prelate:

> "It was necessary for the Synod to speak of the Church as a mystery and communion" because "in spite of the great work the Council had achieved, it did not put enough emphasis on interior conversion and spiritual renewal." "The communion of the Church is not like a cooperative, but it is a reflection on the communion of the Father, Son, and Holy Spirit." "All this must be understood before we turn our attention to the problems of the world."

[9] *Il Tempo*, 4 Dec. 1985, p. 3; 7 Dec.1985, p. 22.

[10] *Ibid.*

In a press conference held at the headquarters of the Augustinian Fathers' generalate, across from the old Holy Office, Bishop Henri Teissier, coajutor of Algiers and president of the Episcopal Conference of Northern Africa, (Algiers, Tunisia, Libya, and Morocco, with some 200,000 faithful, nine bishops, 400 priests and 1200 religious) said a general response to today's relations between Christians and Moslems was not possible.[11]

In his own territory, he attested, the Church was free to carry out its objectives, running schools, clinics, hospitals, shelters, etc. While there are fanatic Moslems intent upon eradicating the Christian presence, they do not present grave difficulties.

In Tunisia, a healthy dialogue is in progress and in black Africa and Asia, where the Moslem and Christian communities are numerically almost equal, there is mutual respect and cooperation in civil and political fields. In the states where Islam is the predominant religion, there is no room for other religions.

As for dialogue, it exists on both the theoretical and practical planes. He had recently attended a symposium on sanctity in the Moslem and Christian tradition, and took part in a moral conference on the ethics of transplants and other medical procedures. True dialogue exists where true friendships have been established.

A fellow bishop admitted that until now he had considered communism as the real threat to Christianity. Now one had to recognize the immense difficulties resulting from Islam and the intolerance of fundamentalist Moslems. Islam is a penetrating force that makes use of all means from the psychological and political to intimidation and violence.

The Maronite patriarch of Lebanon, Cardinal Koraiche spoke frankly of the menace of intolerant Islam. "Not in thirteen centuries has Christianity been confronted with such a menace that is actually planning a campaign to create a theocratic predominance, in which there is no room for Christians."

[11]*Il Tempo*, 3 Dec. 1985, p. 21.

In his special intervention, the retired Cardinal Marty of Paris invited the Synod to manifest the courage that characterized the Council. He said the Church must demonstrate its hope and pass over from fear to faith in a new missionary drive. Missionary dynamism demanded the courage of collegiality lived together with Peter, and in the college of bishops in communion with all the members of the Church, each exercising its own proper but diverse activity.

Cardinal Munoz Vega of Ecuador insisted on a more consistent dialogue between the bishops and theologians that would favor a more faithful interpretation of the doctrine of the Council. He said the Council had exemplified a unique instance of how liberty and unity should be harmonized under the Pope and with the collaboration of the theologians.

And Cardinal Volk of Mainz said the faith diminishes when suffocated by material goods. The Church's problems are not resolved by an automatic transfer of competence from bishops to priests and from priests to the laity, and from men to women . . . the Church becomes more creditable the less it speaks about itself and gives testimony in word and deed to the Truth of Jesus Christ.

During the tedious voting by handwritten ballots on Friday morning, the Venezuelan Cardinal, Rosalio Castillo Lara, president of the papal commission on Canon Law, complained in English about the unhappy mechanism of the Synod's voting system and said he had hoped for something better in a Synod in search of an "Electronic Updating."

As if rising to the bait, Bishop Malone thanked the cardinal for his suggestion, particularly since it was made in English, and said these sentiments echoed the desire of many synodal fathers and would surely have an effect once the prelates returned home. Looking up, in some surprise, the Pope smiled indicating his acquiescence.

5

Implementation (II)

In settling down to the arduous task of small group discussions in language differentiated circles, the ten groups including the prelates specially invited by the Holy Father were asked to answer three questions: What proposals should be submitted to the pope's consideration? What should be done to further the impact of the Council? and What should be the result of the Synod? As it had already been decided that the assembly would issue a Message to the Faithful, should they also prepare a *relatio* or statement of their accomplishments?

When this information was given to the press, some confusion resulted with several journalists claiming that a clash between the Synod and the curia was in the offing, since the latter did not want the Synod to exercise the prerogative of making its own message without previous vetting by the papal office. Actually the matter had been decided earlier at the suggestion of the Canadian Bishop Bernard Hubert and sanctioned by the cardinal presidents.

Work had been started on the message to the faithful by a committee of four including Cardinal Jean Marie Lustiger of Paris and Bishop Castrillon Hoyos of Colombia, the first version being rejected by the assembly as too euphoric, unreal and poetic — in a word, Lustigerian. A fifth man was added to the committee as it settled down to rework the document in keeping with suggestions from the synodal fathers. Refashioned and submitted to a vote paragraph by paragraph in the course of its emendation, the statement was finally accepted by the gathering almost unanimously.

In its Message to the People of God, the Synod asserted that together with the Pope, its members had participated intensely in a privileged moment of communion in prayer, dialogue and study.[1] The result was a confirmation of Vatican II as the light that Christ gives to his followers in each period of history. Insisting that through the church, Christ is present in the midst of the world, they said this was the essence of the mystery revealed in the Christian Message of Salvation.

A more turbulent press reaction greeted the resumes of the small group discussions when it was claimed that the German circle including Cardinals Ratzinger and Höffner, followed by the Latin-speaking contingent — Archbishops Loquang, Padiyara, Thanangathil and Cardinals Palazzini, Sabatini and the octogenarian Vaivods of Lithuania had finally betrayed the obstructive hand of the curial control within the synodal discussions by giving a pessimistic report. *Le Monde* headlined the German resumé *Le Synode change de ton* stating that after the euphoric experience of the first week in praising the merits of the Council, the Synod had now turned to confronting its evil consequences.[2]

The *Le Monde* article indicated that the German contingent had directed a deluge of criticism aimed at the subjectivism now dominating Christian practice; a falling off in the recognition of mankind's obligations before God; a pluralism in scripture interpretation, doctrine and morals that called into question the magisterium of the Church; a lack of theological comprehension; insufficient invoking of the witness of the saints; and a tendency on the part of Catholics to constitute their own Church.

Over against this synopsis, the resumé of the German report in the semi-official handouts and as published in

[1]C. Vinciguerra, *Il Tempo*, 7 Dec. 1985, p. 22.

[2]H. Tinco, *Le Monde*, 5 Dec. 1985, p. 25.

L'Osservatore Romano gave a much more optimistic version:

> The German Language Study Group manifests its gratitude to the Pope for this Extraordinary Synod and totally supports the Council. Its members rejoice that the Synod offers the opportunity to comprehend and live still better the Council.
>
> The Church, as the Council emphasizes, can be understood in her specific form only in relation to the Mystery of Christ.
>
> From this perspective, the Council has spoken of the Church in a marvelous way. The German Language Study Group asks itself to what extent this richness has brought forth fruit in their regions over the last twenty years.
>
> The reasons — internal and external — for the distress which often manifests itself in the Church have been examined. The group itself sought to make an examination of conscience. Has there not perhaps been too much talk of the Church and not enough of Christ? In the Church's pastoral opening to the world, has use been made of overcritical worldly categories and points of reference? In liturgical celebrations, has the value of reverance, of the sacred and of silence been sufficiently taken into account? Have the major post-conciliar pastoral instructions of the papal magisterium (e.g., on catechesis, on work, on the family) been sufficiently drawn upon for the actualization of the Council?
>
> Concrete suggestions were provided as to how the conciliar texts can be known, assimilated and lived. It was also emphasized that preaching, catechesis and pastoral work must stress the real problems of mankind today, and not merely the themes prevalent in the attention of the day; themes that in the last analysis fail to grasp the most profound problems of man, and especially of the young.
>
> The Synod must give a message of encouragement and hope. However, Christian hope is different from pure optimism; it sees reality clearly (which is obviously different from pessimism!)

> It is conscious of the fact that Christ has already been victorious, and that he will lead us too, through participation in his Cross, towards total fullness. [3]

Actually the truth of the matter lay somewhere between the two resumes. The six page report itself asserted unhesitatingly the majestic truth of the Mystery of the Church living within the shadow of the Trinity. That it then turned to a show of concern for its blemishes and the remedies was considered a germanic trait.

The French group A including Cardinal Lustiger of Paris and Monsignor Philippe Delhaye, head of the papal theological commission, together with a number of francophone African prelates and Oriental patriarchs had also felt the need to denounce post-conciliar abuses and prescribe corrective measures. In particular they deplored the abandonment of the sacrament of penance and errors in catechetical instruction and stated that false feminist pretensions should be resisted. As reported in the English version of the *L'Osservatore Romano,* they asserted:

> 1. The mystery of Christ is always actualized by the Church. This allows men to be in contact with the Word of Jesus and the power of Grace.
>
> The Church is essentially a hierarchical communion. Sacramental grace is not to be confused with organizations. The essential structures link men with Christ, the Apostles and their successors, in particular with Peter and the Pope.
>
> Towards other religions the Church wishes to have an attitude of receptivity, recognizing some of their values. Still, she cannot fail to preach that Christ is the one Saviour.
>
> The preferential but not exclusive option for the poor is an evangelical requirement which asserts itself in a special way in our day. It must not, however, be polluted by political options.
>
> 2. As regards the Council itself, the group shares the clear and optimistic evaluation of the Synod. In some

[3] *L'Oss. Rom.* (Eng.), 16 Dec. 1985, all the resumes are taken from the same issue.

> regions, it is still a question of making the Council known. In others, a critical evaluation is necessary. Still, it is better to witness to the Christian values that Vatican II has professed than to get involved in exclusively negative polemics and criticisms.

As cited in *Le Monde,* Monsignor Delhaye had also taken exception to certain episcopal conferences who, he said, were demonstrating "a feudal, regional vision of the Church" that in his view threatened the power of Rome. Originally a conciliar theologian in the cortege of the Johannine Cardinal Suenens, Delhaye seemed to have taken a Ratzingerian twist backwards.

The Italian language groups were also reported to have deplored the loss of the sense of sin among Catholics and the profanation of the Sunday with the overstress on commercial and sport activity. As reported in the semi-official resumé by Cardinal Dadaglio, the Church's Grand Penitentiary, they said:

> After a rapid consideration of the gravest problems, pains, anxieties and hopes of the modern world, Christian and non-Christian, they unanimously recognized the necessity of promoting the knowledge of Vatican II by means of a "Catechism of the Faith" directed towards believers; a "Book of the Christian Faith" offered to non-believers; and a "Book of Moral Doctrine" for everyone. They desired a more explicit and exact knowledge of the "collegiality of the bishops with the Pope" in the Church; of the doctrinal, sacramental and disciplinary communion of the particular Churches with the Pope and under the guidance of the Pope. They insisted on the infallibility in faith and morals promised by Christ to the Church, assisted by the Holy Spirit, and guaranteed by the Pope, as an expression of the Church even in the ordinary magisterium exercised by him and by the bishops in union with him.
>
> They likewise called for the precise elucidation of the bishops' responsibilities in the spiritual, doctrinal and human formation of priests; in the integration of reli-

> gious life in the apostolate of the particular Churches; and in the promotion of the laity in their ecclesial formation and in their responsibilities. All these prerogatives were recognized by the Christocentric ecclesiology of Vatican II.
>
> They further proposed the promotion of the "theology of the liturgy" in order to enrich the religious and sacramental life of the people of God; and they deplored vain ritualism and presumptuous and uncontrolled personal creativity.
>
> Finally, they called for a positive conclusion to the Synod, with precise adherence to Vatican Council II and to the Magisterium (ordinary as well) of the Pope; and the formulation of concrete "propositions" concerning the religious, moral and social problems of the Church and the world, to be elaborated — if, when and in the manner that the Holy Father deems opportune — in an eventual Apostolic Exhortation.

The subservience of this statement referring to the pope in at least ten instances betrayed the type of papolatry and courtly Byzantinism criticized in the *Civiltà Cattolica* article.

Under the guidance of Bishop Jose Gottardi Cristelli of Uruguay, the Spanish speaking circle proposed the need:

> To emphasize the role of the Church as mystery: the active presence of Christ in her that culminates in the Liturgy. From the Cross he communicates the paschal and holy life to us. Only sanctity is the root and guarantee of the integral conversion of the Church (including her structures and her relationship with the world).
>
> On church-world relationship they asserted that: the major problems that constitute scandal for the Christian conscience were discussed (misery, attacks on human rights, monopolies, the arms race, world division according to ideologies and North-South relations); and they emphasized the need to give human (moral) meaning to technical-scientific progress, and to proceed with the interpretation of the new signs of the times (GS 91).

In a typical gallic approach the group in the French language circle B asserted:

> The Synod must ask itself the question: what is the mission of the Church today? The notion of communion and collegiality must be deepened from this perspective. Also proposed is the idea of a permanent structure in the Church with the task of actualizing the Council.
>
> Among the initiatives to be undertaken at the level of the particular Churches are the need to keep in mind in the spreading of the Council's texts the portion of humanity that cannot read or write. The Church must seriously commit herself to the study of the new problems posed by the biological and human sciences, in order to bring her evangelical witness into this environment; and may the dignity of women be recognized and promoted with concrete actions in the church and the world.

In the English language study group A reported by Cardinal Francis Arinze of the Curia:

> The key concept of "communio" must be reflected by structures and relationships within the Church. These should protect unity of faith and charity while promoting the pluriformity of the Spirit's gifts. The Church, having received truth and love in Christ must communicate these to the world.
>
> The Church should constantly heed the call to holiness. Authentic spiritual formation is needed. So that the Church may more readily respond to the Word, Christian unity should remain a major priority. The work of the Secretariat for Christian Unity is so important that it should be raised to the status of a Congregation of the Curia.

As reported by Archbishop Gregorios Thanangathil, the Latin study group said:

> The Fathers applaud the liturgical reform but felt that the rapid rhythm with which it was carried out produced a certain loss of the sense of the sacred. This must be

restored along with the forms of private devotion.

The Fathers also indicate the correlation between evangelization and the sacraments, which are not in opposition but complete one another. They have particularly considered the sacraments of the Eucharist and Penance.

In commenting on the Constitution of the Church, they focused attention on the principle of subsidiarity to be clarified so as to avoid incorrect interpretations.

In the international assemblies promoted in defense of human dignity, may Christians, in every way possible, recall the right of every individual to the free profession of his faith.

In promoting ecclesiastical discipline, charity cannot be weakness on the part of those who perform the service of authority. Even the threat of ecclesiastical punishment is, in the intent of the legislator, an exercise of charity towards those who are in error.

On Thursday evening of the second week a Prayer Service for Christian Unity was conducted by the Holy Father and the non-Catholic Observers to which the synodal fathers were participants. Speaking in the name of the ecumenical groups which he said were not homogeneous in beliefs, the tall, dignified, former dean of Christ's Church, Oxford, and a foremost Anglican theologian, Professor Henry Chadwick delivered an address:

> You have generously invited us, as representatives of Churches and Christian World Communions with whom the Roman Catholic Church is in active dialogue, to be Observers at this Synod, thereby renewing the experience of Vatican II. You have not seen us to be outsiders or rivals, and we have not felt ourselves to be so. You have received us as brothers in Christ through faith and baptism, though not yet in perfect communion. Observers are not detached spectators: we are deeply engaged in your discussion. All Christian bodies face the need for reconciliation of diversity and unity, the testing of our moral judgement in face of modern scientific advances,

and the challenges of atheism and secularism.

We admire the fearless courage with which the Synod looks into the future, especially in places where Christians are few, poor, or persecuted. In listening to those who have spoken from such places we have heard echoes of our own situation too.

We have rejoiced to hear solid support for the work of the Second Vatican Council. The emphasis placed, both at Vatican II and in this Synod, on communion (koinonia) as a key to the understanding of the nature of the Church is important for ecumenism. This communion is created for us, not by us: it draws us to the Father in Christ through the Holy Spirit.

We also share the Synod's concerns both for the primacy of repentance and the spiritual life, and for justice, peace and the poor.

The Synod has made it very clear that ecumenism is an essential part of the way forward, and that it does not involve a betrayal of divine truth and faith. Those who have taken an active part in it know that it requires patience, attentive listening, and much toil. There are bound to be moments of discouragement.

In his response the Holy Father said:

Dear Brothers and Sisters,

There is one center around which the human family can be united — Jesus Christ. That is the will and plan of God.

Divisions among Christians are contrary to the plan of God. "There is one God, and there is one mediator between God and men, the man Christ Jesus" (1 Tim 2:5), in whom God wishes to reconcile all things to himself. Those who are the bearers of his mission must themselves be reconciled; they must show forth his unifying love in action; they must live in that communion which is towards the Father through the Son in the Holy Spirit, and they must manifest this in a united community which witnesses to the reconciling work of God.

The Second Vatican Council threw new light on this imperative and the present Synod has reaffirmed it. So it

> was important that in these days, in company with our friends the delegated Observers from the other Churches and Christian World Communions, we should spend some time in prayer for the unity of Christians.
>
> The restoration of unity must be above all a restoration of the inner dimension of the Christian life - a whole-hearted personal commitment to Jesus Christ which makes intolerable any separation among those who share that commitment. Any faltering in the movement towards unity since the impetus of the Second Vatican Council is partly due to the fact that we have not attended enough to this interior dimension. We must not take it for granted.

The following morning after the recitation of the canonical hour of Terce, the lay observers presented their considerations. Sr. Katherine MacDonald, Superior General of the Sisters of Our Lady of Sion spoke for the religious sisters and brothers in the groups of lay observers and Mr. Thibor Sulik, a Brazilian Labor leader, for the laity.

After thanking the Holy Father for the privilege of being present at the Synod, Sr. Katherine said: "The Synod has given us not only an experience of the Universal Church, but also an occasion for meditating with you on the mystery and sacrament of the Church to which we belong by virtue of baptism, although our group lives its ecclesial life in two specific vocations: the common life of the convent and the monastery and the vast group of the faithful living in the world.

Commenting on the recent decrease in vocations to the religious life, Sr. Katherine said that young people were again entering in increasing numbers on some continents though more slowly, in others. Noting that the Synod spoke continually of "communion" she remarked that by the renewal of structures and ways of relating to one another, the religious communities were once more striving to give encouragement to people in a world where individualism and materialism are rampant.

"The lay members of our group" she admitted, "want to see in us a paradigm of the Christian life of love and service."

They want us truly inserted in the world that is ours today, there to witness to a life freely assumed and lived according to our vows — a witness to the Absolute of God."

In turn Mr. Sulik commented on the privilege of being part of the Synod and the realization it gave the group of the universal dimension of the Church within the diversity of ethnic cultures.

All the values of the doctrine of Vatican Council II have been reaffirmed and maintained even if in many regions it may not have been sufficiently transmitted among the Christian people.

Of the great achievements of the Council, its openness to the outside world has been most encouraging. Dialogue has been almost globally established as we have experienced during this Synod. This dialogue in today's world is most important. Only man is capable of dialogue, of communicating with others, of listening with patience, love and even sacrifice, avoiding that confrontation which has its roots in selfishness, and which generates violence.

He acknowledged the fact that "the immense task of confronting the world's evils from hunger, the cancer of the arms race, economic and social inequalities, racial and religious forms of discrimination, falls to us laity who must undertake the renewal of the temporal order as our responsibility." He said the Church had a right to expect a lively witness from its faithful "because all of creation is good, placed at the disposal of all mankind, according to the mandate of the Creator."

Finally he remarked: "We have witnessed the wide ranging debates promoted within civil society regarding the advancement of women. We believe that just such an authentic advancement is necessary. Women contribute immeasurably to all areas of human activity. The Church has need of this contribution."

Meanwhile work had been started on the Synod's final *relatio* or statement of proposals. As described by Cardinal Danneels it was not to be the work of a committee of experts. Rather the document was to evolve out of the interventions of the first four days and the reports of the small language groups as recorded by professor Kasper and several theologians invited by the Holy Father including the noted Swiss scholar Hans Urs von Balthasar.

Submitted to emendation paragraph by paragraph, the document finally met with the group's voted approval despite several non-placet votes and abstentions. Attempts to label the *relatio* a curial document influenced by the Ratzinger pessimism were refuted by a careful reading of the document. It did manifestly deal with the light and shadows experienced by the Church in the post-conciliar age; and it did confront the problems challenging the church today from within and outside. But its tone and statements were not merely positive but, for the most part, euphoric. And instead of being addressed solely to the Holy Father as proposals for his consideration, the *relatio* was published with his explicit consent as *The Church in the Word of God celebrates the mysteries of Christ for the Salvation of the World.* It is no wonder that Cardinal Danneels called this document a precedent setting achievement in synodal development that cannot be reversed.[4]

Dealing with the Mystery of the Church, the Sacred Liturgy, the Church as Communion, and the Mission of the Church in the World, the document insisted that while the signs of the times today differ from those of twenty years ago, the authenticity of the Council remains unaffected. Its documents are to be read critically and put into effect conjointly so that a renewed vision of the Church may be achieved by the third millennium.

While it maintained that it was erroneous to separate pastoral from doctrinal concerns, the document confirmed the autonomy of temporal affairs and the need to accept secularization without the idolotries of materialism, consumerism and hedonism. In restoring the sense of mystery and the sacred to the Church, the Synod proved itself a Christocentric achievement. It was accepted by the Holy Father without emendations. So was the reconfirmation of the 15 prelates who constituted the Council of the Secretary General of the Synod, for the Synod of 1983, with the task of

[4]See Appendix II.

overseeing the implementation of the last Synod and preparing the agenda of the next ordinary Synod to be held in 1986. By the Synodal rule the committee that had prepared the way for the present Extraordinary Synod should have ceased to exist and been replaced by a new group. In spite of canon law, a request was made by Bishop Jean Vilnet of Lille that the current group be retained since they were so heavily involved in preparations for the Synod on the Laity now postponed until 1987.[5]

Some uncertainty surrounded the matter not merely because of synodal regulations but because as Giancarlo Zizola pointed out, at the Synod of 1983 on Penance and Reconciliation, a majority of the delegates feeling frustrated at their inability to publish a statement of their own making, had elected twelve of their members who had been most outspoken in their synodal interventions. They included Cardinals Bernardin of Chicago, Martini of Milan, Sin of Manila, Ballestrero of Turin, Arns of São Paulo and Lorscheider of Fortaleza, Brazil. After a brief hesitation, the Holy Father had decided to accept their election but immediately added three archconservative prelates, Cardinals Ratzinger of the curia, Lopez Trujillo of Medellin, Bogota, and the Ukrainian Archbishop Hermaniuk of Winnipeg.[6]

In the light of this circumstance it was thought that the curia would insist on the rule eliminating the men not present at the current Synod, *viz* Bernardin, Martini, Sin, Arns, and Trujillo. But papal acquiescence to the request was immediately forthcoming.

Some surprise was registered earlier on at the absence of the cardinal of Milan from the Synod, since he was considered a close confidant of the Pope. Rumors had it that he had displeased John Paul by his stance on Reconciliation but there was no evidence for the supposition.

On Saturday morning, during the final session of the Synod, the Holy Father delivered an address to the gather-

[5]Cf. *Il Tempo*, 7 Dec. 1985, p. 22. The members were: Cardinals Bernadin, Arns, Cordeiro, Sin, Zoungrana, Lorscheider, Hume, Etchegaray, Trujillo, Martini, Ratzinger, Archbishops Hermaniuk, Naidoo and Bishops Teissier and Hamao.

[6]G. Zizola, *Restaurazione,* p. 1675.

ing in which for all practical purposes he gave a summary of the final *relatio*.

After profusely thanking by name and service all and sundry who had contributed to "this joyful and highly spiritual experience" including those who "worked behind the scenes and were never seen," the Holy Father said:

> I express my real gratitude to all of you who have taken part in this assembly of the Second Extraordinary Synod of Bishops. A particular grace for all has been the fraternal presence of the Observer-Delegates of the other Churches and Communities. Your presence here calls to mind the provident ecclesial act between Rome and Constantinople which took place twenty years ago; after the conclusion of the Council. With a parallel and contemporary celebration in Saint Peter's Basilica and in the Church of Saint George at the Phanar in Istanbul there was published the common declaration of Pope Paul VI and the Patriarch Athenagoras I of venerated memory, with which it was decreed that there should be removed from the memory and the life of the Church the sentences of *anathema* inflicted in 1054 which constituted a sign of schism and a true impediment to reconciliation in charity...
>
> Gradually there was removed from minds the memory of a past marked by a pugnacious and contentious spirit; charity has grown stronger and the spirit of reconciliation has been confirmed. For all these reasons, that event remains emblematic of the will which must inspire the entire question of the unity of Christians: namely mutual pardon which grows and expresses itself in fraternal charity. From here emerge all the initiatives of research and dialogue, the activities for the restoration of complete unity.
>
> The memory of that event urges us on to renew that original spirit since we must continue, widen, and increase our common efforts to restore unity, in order to be faithful to the will of the Lord concerning his Church.
>
> Twenty years after the conclusion of the Council this

> common assembly appeared necessary, indeed absolutely demanded, after the great and vast heritage of the Ecumenical Council of Vatican II. It was necessary that at this moment, above all those who were called to take part in it, express their judgement on Vatican II in order to avoid divergent interpretations.
>
> The results of your work — contained in the Message and in the final *relatio* — are a witness to your clearsightedness and your diligent care as well as to your fine *sensus ecclesiae*. I wish also to underline another characteristic of this assembly of the Synod: variety in unity. The Fathers were able to express their thoughts freely. The interventions made in the Hall and in the small discussion groups were deserving of appreciation. But this liberty was in no way an obstacle to the substantial unity. In this way you manifested collegial spirit in an excellent way.
>
> With joy and with sincere gratitude I accept from your hands the Message and the final *relatio* which demonstrate this sense of communion. With my consent these documents will be made public.

He asserted that the Synod had given unquestionable testimony to the Church's catholicity. Convoked in the Synod were persons from every continent belonging to different cultures but professing the same faith ... In a particular manner, the Synod examined the nature of the Church as a Mystery and a communion, that is a "*Koinonia*"... There has been likewise a renewed stress on the collegial nature of the episcopate: the bishops, as Vatican II says "are not only consecrated for one diocese alone but for the whole world." Thus the episcopal office extends and in some manner participates more fully in the ministry of guiding the universal church.

Citing the desire of many prelates that a compendium or catechism of Catholic doctrine be prepared as a point of reference for catechisms in all the local churches, the Holy Father said the desire represented a real need.

He acquiesced likewise in the need for deeper study of the nature of Episcopal conferences "which in our time offer a precious contribution to the life of the Church." Finally he stated the need for publication of the Code of Canon Law for the Oriental Churches in keeping with their traditions and the decisions of Vatican Council II.

In the end he said he was convinced that the Synod was a particularly useful time for the pastoral life of the parishes, religious communities, the dioceses, Oriental Church synods and the Bishops Conferences.

Cardinal Krol had the last word. After giving profuse thanks to all the participants and reminding the assembly of the aims entrusted to them by the Holy Father, he said:

"First of all, we have celebrated and relived the experience of communion that characterized the period of the Council. We cannot help but rejoice over the overwhelming spirit of collegiality, community, and friendly exchange that filled the Synod Hall and the linguistic groups. Was this not a gift of the Spirit who helped us to follow the Lord's injunction at the Last Supper to love one another as he has loved us?

"Then we verified the progress made in living the Council in the varied and rich diversity of so many local situations ... This unity in diversity gave the impression of forming a magnificent mosaic in which the pieces are composed of varied experiences of communion, of collegial feeling and action, of liturgical adaptation, of the transmission of faith, of evangelization, of inculturation, of social doctrine.

This rich experience of communion has served to free us for a broader sense of the needs of the universal Church from a narrow concentration on national points of view ...

This situation as we have seen, comprises a felicitious abundance of efforts and resolutions to implement the Council; however there were not lacking certain upsets and difficulties which followed later, though in no way deriving their origin from the Council.

Citing Pope John's exhortation at the start of the Council: "The Church must keep in mind new situations, new forms of life that open up new ways for the Catholic apostolate ... Ours is not the task of guarding this sacred treasure as if it were a museum piece, but to apply it fearlessly, courageously to the needs of our time . . ." the Philadelphia cardinal said:

"Our final hope and wish is that — in the words of Peter in his First Letter — we may remain in the love of the brotherhood, and may carefully and sincerely love one another."

On this note of amity and fraternal love, the Synod came to a graceful end.

6

Postscript

Pope John Paul's Extraordinary Synod of Bishops ended with the pageantry of a Pontifical concelebrated Mass preceded by a panoply of cardinals, oriental prelates, bishops and monsignori in their colorful hieratic garb, who marched across the Piazza fronting on St. Peter's and down the vast aisle of the basilica to take their places in the four serrated tribunes facing the papal altar beneath the Baldachino of Bernini.

Celebrated in Latin with choir and faithful chanting the Gregorian *Missa de Angelis* in alternating verses, the solemn Liturgy proved a nostalgic as well as a moving experience for most of the participants including the diplomatic corps, journalists and photographers, television and radio crews and a throng of visitors fortunate enough to have obtained a *biglietto* from the Vatican visitors bureau.

In his homily delivered in Latin, John Paul made fulsome reference to the Immaculate Conception of the Blessed Virgin Mary, the liturgical feast of the day. Commenting on the Synod's edifying achievement, the Holy Father said:

> The Synod has accomplished the purpose for which it was convened: to celebrate, verify and promote the Council.
>
> As we come out of the Synod, we wish to intensify our pastoral efforts and ensure that the Second Vatican

> Council is more widely and more thoroughly known; to ensure that the orientations and directives that the Council left us are assimilated into the heart of all the members of the People of God, and translated into the way they live with consistency and love.
>
> At the end of this eucharistic celebration the Message which the Synod Fathers are addressing to the Church and the world will be proclaimed in various languages. I hope this message will touch all hearts, strengthening everyone's commitment to putting into generous and consistent practice the teachings and directives of the Second Vatican Council. [1]

Among the first to render judgment on the Synod was Archbishop Jan Schotte, Secretary General of the Synodal Council, who in a final press conference on Monday with several hundred journalists in attendance, acknowledged their role in making the assembly a global event. He said the information dispensed in the *sala stampa* and dispersed through the press seemed good and faithful although he was aware of several flights of fancy that did not reflect the truth of what had been said and done.

As for the Synod itself Schotte said that it had been a very open process: "A Synod is not a political parliament that has particular interests to protect; nor was it a predetermined or planned procedure if only because it involved some 160 independent-minded bishops who could not be controlled beforehand ... It was a process of dialogue, of listening, of a presentation of openness and ideas in full liberty ...

Every assembly, he continued, has something diverse and unrepeatable. This was a truly extraordinary assembly in that it did not produce a confrontation or unhappy quarrels.

Asked about liberation theology he said yes it was discussed but not often, and in fact emphasis was placed more on the integral liberation of the individual and the role

[1] *L'Oss. Rom.* (Eng.), 16 Dec., pp. 1-4.

which we are called to play in life. But this of course was another subject.

He thus ignored the play between the two Latin American factions within the Synod and the complaints of curial intransigence made by a number of bishops in the Synod as well as in interviews with the press.

Asked about the significance of the universal catechism, he said this was not meant as a restrictive measure against the independent teaching faculty of the bishop, since such a compendium would be about the faith where there is no room for differences of opinion. This statement was hardly in keeping with the testimony of theological pluralism exemplified in the Synod and justified by the Church's tradition down the ages.[2]

On his way north, Cardinal Danneels at the request of the archbishop of Milan, Cardinal Carlo Martini, whose absence from the Synod had been noted, stopped off to give the Milanese clergy a first hand account of the synodal doings. As described by *La Repubblica,* he was dressed in clergyman — black suit and Roman collar rather than pontifical cassock — with only a small pectoral cross and chain to denote his eminent rank.[3]

In his discourse, Danneels stressed the part played by the third world prelates in the synodal discussions saying they had brought a new and important element into the Church's self-image. These bishops had insisted on the theology of the Cross that had been touched upon but not deepened by the Council. They thus created a climate of conscious sympathy for the persecuted churches. And he cited Bulgaria, Hungary, Czechoslovakia, Vietnam and Cambodia. The latter's bishop had said Catholics in his country were totally deprived of priests and religious. If the Churches of Silence have had so much attention in the final *relatio,* he said, this is due to the fact that "in the East, love for the Church is

[2]*Avvenire*, 10 Dec. 1985, p. 10.

[3]*La Reppublica*, 10 Dec. 1985, p. 4.

much stronger than elsewhere; there the Church is much better received."

Acknowledging the fact that some critics were claiming that the final *relatio* was a series of compromises revealing the power of the Ratzinger curialists, the Belgian cardinal defended the document as an authentic and independent complement to the achievements of the Council. "All the post-conciliar periods in the past," he affirmed, "were eras of great tension. We can ask ourselves whether without the Council, there would not have been a crumbling of the dikes."

Referring to current difficulties he said that only one third of the bishops at the Synod had been at the Council; and he doubted whether many of the two thirds had found the time to study its documents with care. One bishop had complained to him that there was too much material and wanted a synthesis; "but how," he asked, "do you synthesize a Council?"

In discussing the polemics surrounding the Synod's decision in favor of a universal catechism, the cardinal said he was of the opinion that such a catechism was not possible in today's world.

The Church was not living in the restricted world of the Council of Trent. With the considerable opposition of many hierarchies to the notion of such a catechism it would be better to consider a compendium as a book of reference.

Danneels also revealed the fact that in the beginning the Holy Father was opposed to the composition of a final *relatio*. "The Council is what it is" he quoted John Paul as saying, "What can I possibly add to it?" But the insistence of so many bishops had achieved a change on the pontiff's part. "And now that the results of the synodal debate have been made public," he insisted, "this constitutes a precedent from which there can be no turning back." In this sense he considered the Synod a definite success.

Asked by Cardinal Martini "What then remains of the Council," he replied, "An African bishop told me his problem was not religious liberty, but the difficulty he had in explaining to his people why Christ was not black."

In an offhand, pejorative report in the *National Catholic Reporter,* Peter Hebblethwaite quarreled with the final report as obviously overinfluenced by the Ratzinger thesis of the need of the Church for doctrinal and disciplinary surveillance. He was critical of the imprecision revealed in the language employed in the documents, maintaining that the Synod lacked the assistance of competent theologians such as had graced the Council.

In the same paper, Arthur Jones wrote about the vicissitudes of the Oriental rite prelates whose grievances against both the Roman curia and the persecuting nations were aired both in and outside the Synod. He held out little hope for their ecclesial betterment despite the soon to be published Oriental code of canon law.

The *Wanderer's* Philip Trower felt that of the three most important results of the assembly, the proposal to create a universal catechism was the most significant. "Modernism," he said, "has been resisting the idea of such a catechism for years." The second most significant result, he maintained, was the prelates' admission that the Council, while never teaching error, was not in every point absolutely flawless. In one of their most startling admissions, the Synod prelates stated that "In no way can it be affirmed that everything that took place after the Council was inspired by the Council."

Finally, he felt that the prelates recognized that at almost every level and in almost every sphere of Catholic life the presentation of the Faith had been disastrously desupernaturalized.

By way of comment on this startling accusation, Trower wondered whether God "had not allowed the fundamentalist sects which the synodal Fathers are so worried about to prosper for a time, in order to get this idea across.[4]

In his analysis of the Synod's results Gian Franco Svidercoschi in *Il Tempo* said that the Synod was actually a rereading of the Council, stressing its new orientation, its problems and priorities.

Today, he said, the synodal fathers had a great advantage

[4]*The Wanderer*, 19 Dec. 1985., p. 8.

over the Council's prelates. They were not burdened by the conditions that surrounded the conciliar debates and their aftermath, that had weighed so heavily on the documents and their immediate interpretation over the past two decades.[5]

He claimed that the Council had rediscovered the true meaning of the Church's tradition, purifying it of all the rigidities and burdensome superstructure that the sixteenth century counter-Reformation and the long confrontation between the Church and the world had imposed on it.

As an example of this achievement he cited *Lumen Gentium,* the dogmatic Constitution on the Church in which the Council turned attention on the Church's own inner nature and its mission only to discover that while seen as principally an institution hierarchically and juridically organized, it was rather a Mystery of Faith and Salvation as defined in the Gospels. In returning to the mystery of the sacred, to the cross, and to mystical communion in the *koinonia,* the Church through the Synod had rediscovered its authentic image.

Declaring the report issued by the bishops a compromise, Kenneth Briggs in the *New York Times* said it balanced liberal and traditionalist themes that were in contention during the synodal debates. Among the issues raised by conservatives were the need for ending what it called abuses in the liturgy and theology, infusing a greater sense of "mystery" into the Church and restoring authority in the highest levels of the hierarchy centering on the pope.

At the same time liberals emphasized the need to strengthen decision making at the local level and to accept theological diversity and openness to change in Church discipline.[6]

In a realistic report to the faithful of his archdiocese Cardinal Basil Hume of Westminster, England, told them "There will be no immediate changes next week because of the fortnight of discussion by the bishops in the presence of

[5]*Ii Tempo*, 7 Dec. 1985, p. 22.

[6]*New York Times*, 9 Dec. 1985.

the pope . . . But there is a message that is important for Catholics in their parishes."

There is now a road mapped out for the future; there is an indication of how we are to move closer to the other Christian churches.[7]

He admitted that, not surprisingly, there were no great achievements from the fortnight's work. The bishops in Rome, he said, admitted realistically that there is still a long way to go before the teachings of the Council enter fully into our Catholic blood stream.

Speaking of the Church as a *koinonia* of mystical communion, that had been the burden of the cardinal's intervention at the Synod, Hume said that the concept of the Church as *communio* linked it to the Trinity, helped in the search for Christian unity, gave richer significance to the Eucharist, and embraced the Cross as the sign of Christ's passion, death and resurrection. Here we begin to make sense of the agony of life when illness and persecution are seen in a special way as part of the mystery of the Cross.

In his reflections on the Synod, Monsignor George Higgins sympathized with the reporters and professional Vaticanologists while criticizing their hope that the assembly would furnish them with exciting copy in a battle between progressives and traditionalists by tackling the ordination of women to the priesthood, clerical celibacy, nuclear warfare, apartheid and related issues. Saying that these matters were too important to be discussed in a two-week Synod, he felt the real result of the Synod was a sense of hope for the future, a word of encouragement for Christians committed to the letter and the spirit of Vatican II.

In *Commonweal,* Peter Steinfels claimed that in Ratzinger the liberals had found an ally *malgré lui.* He said out loud what the Curia believes but prefers to keep quiet. The German cardinal thus proffered the liberals a target.[8]

In providing an explanation for the post-conciliar upsets

[7]*Tablet*, 14 Dec. 1985, pp. 1023-1024.

[8]Cf. P. Steinfels, "So far, so good, so what"; *Commonweal*, 20 Dec. 1985, pp. 698-700.

and dissidence, Steinfels maintained it was due mainly to the "frequently half-hearted, uncomprehending, begrudging and authoritarian" implementation by the pope and bishops.

Whereas the Council had "enrolled Catholicism in a crash course in modernity . . . the Church's leadership let much of its creditability drain away as it balked, scolded and seemed to ignore much of the Council's vision." It was this fact that the Synod had ignored, thus failing to come to grips in its proposals with the curia's peremptory and unilateral decisions that so disturbed so many of the bishops and faithful looking to Rome for a *communio* of love and understanding in their confrontation of a hostile world within and outside the Church.

In his summation, Steinfels admitted the Synod, despite its omissions, was not a setback. Its concern for collegiality would probably not affect Rome's use of its power of appointment, its censures and pressure on bishops and religious. Nevertheless it had encouraged the majority of the bishops to pursue their current endeavors to make the conciliar Church an actuality among their faithful and clergy. This was a major achievement.

In a press conference immediately after the final session, Bishop Malone, president of the U.S. Bishops Conference, said the Synod had been an unqualified success. To Catholics who have accepted the Council's enrichment of the liturgy, greater fraternity in worship and insertion in various parish activities, he said, the bishops can declare,

> "The good news from the Synod is that you have been doing all the right things!"
>
> "To those, however, who have looked askance at liturgical and ecumenical change, who still see worship in terms of a 'solitary communion with God' to the exclusion of neighbor, the bishops must now explain the Council's teaching in a more convincing fashion."[9]

[9] *Long Island Catholic*, 12 Dec.1985, p. 9; cf. *Origins*, 12 Dec.1985, pp. 429-431.

Quoting the pope's statement that Bishops Conferences were "a precious contribution to the life of the Church," Malone said, "That's exactly what I and others asked for."

Those looking for signs of division in the Synod's reports, he went on,

> should remember that the Synod worked by consensus.
> Some of the questions made by individuals on specific pastoral and collegial issues were"winnowed out"during the group discussions. Among them were appeals to consider allowing divorced and remarried Catholics to participate in the sacraments and the request to establish in the Vatican a permanent Synod with legislative powers.

In a final note he said, "The Synod's report focused more on the Person of Christ than on the Church of Christ; and added, "It's a Christocentric document and I believe it is an ecumenical plus."

This observation was unexpected. A theologian had criticised the gathering on this very point remarking that for all the emphasis of the Church as Mystery, on the Sacred, and on the theology of the Cross in the discussions, insufficient attention had been given to the Person of Christ as the center of that Mystery and the embodiment of the Truth that is the Church's heritage.

Likewise there had been little attempt to analyze the nature of the love that is to permeate the life of the Christian, particularly in view of the disagreements within the Church community that had occasioned such scandal within and outside the Church, and in relation to the repressive actions of the Curia.

In the thinking of this theologian, the Synod had served as a smoke screen behind which the participants had taken refuge instead of confronting these two fundamental issues.

Actually two paragraphs in the *relatio* dealt with the presence of Christ as the center of the Church. They insisted that the Son of God is the new Adam revealing both the mystery of God and the mystery of man and his supreme vocation [II, 2-3].[10]

On the issue of the nature of Truth the critic pointed to the obsession attributed to the Prefect of the Congregation for the Doctrine of the Faith in regard to revealed Truth which he and his cohorts insist is contained in propositions drawn from the Scriptures and embodied in tradition via a series of strict logical deductions that are referred to as the *depositum fidei* or the deposit of faith.

The trouble with this concept of revealed truth is that it does not take cognizance of the fact that Christ proclaimed his own Person as the "Way, the Truth and the Life" thus making revealed truth a person and not merely a concatenation of ideas.

In his critique of this scholastic theologizing vis-à-vis the older patristic Christology, Henri (Cardinal) de Lubac wrote:

> The object of the faith is thus emaciated and all but pulverized. It is no longer God who revealed himself and his design of salvation. And man must adhere to a list of truths that in no way assures him in anticipation that he can have an essential bond among them or with himself.
>
> In the end the dogma finds itself in this way totally exteriorized, cut off from its purpose, and the faith tends to be nothing more than a blind submission to a *locutio Dei authoritive docentis* — a word of God teaching authoritatively. [11]

Nor does it pay sufficient attention to the fact that the epistemology used in interpreting the Scriptures is fashioned out of a particular culture, giving rise to diverse schools of theology as has been the case down the ages. This problem was acknowledged by the Council in its decree on the Scriptures (*Dei Verbum)* and is presently

[10]Cf. Appendix II.

[11]H. de Lubac, *La Rivelazione divina e il senso dell' uomo* (Milan, Jaca Book, 1985); cf. *La rivelazione cristiana nella costituzione, "Dei Verbum," Civiltà Cattolica*, 7 Dec. 1985, pp. 417-428.

involved in the call for inculturation particularly on the part of the younger churches.

It is this consideration that stands behind the editorial in *Civiltà Cattolica:*

> It is legitimate to ask whether contemporary Catholics possess the capacity to easily distinguish in the camp of defined truth, the object of the faith from its sociotheologic envelope. This is as much as to say that the precious evangelical element can be separated from the rational-historical process. The latter always respects experience and the values of a certain epoch, and can possibly not be any longer the envelope that can best describe and transmit the evangelical pearl. [12]

The second element was the nature of love as proclaimed by Christ in his command, "Love your neighbor as yourself."

St. Paul has given a magnificent exposition of love in chapter 13 of his first Letter to the Corinthians: "Love is patient and kind; love is not jealous, or conceited, or proud, or selfish, or irritable or ill-mannered; love does not keep a record of wrongs; love is not happy with evil, but is happy with the truth" (4-6).

In keeping with this declaration, Pope John in his inaugural talk at the first session of the Council said: "The Church has always opposed errors ... Frequently she has condemned them with the greatest severity ... Nowadays however, the Spouse of Christ prefers to make use of the medicine of mercy rather than that of severity. She considers that she meets the needs of the present day by demonstrating the validity of her teaching rather than by condemnations ..."

[12] *Civiltà Cattolica*, 2 Nov. 1985, p. 212.

This conviction seemed to have been lost in the recent inquisitional tactics of the Congregation for the Faith and other curial offices, in the censoring of theologians, cautions to bishops and religious, and the comfort given to archconservative zealots continually delating clerics, nuns and other apostles to the Holy See.

At the Synod this latter attitude was manifestly that of the cardinal of Rio de Janeiro who demanded that action be taken when dubeity of belief or practice was discovered. It was given voice in the report of the Latin language circle that said: "In promoting ecclesiastical discipline, charity cannot be weakness on the part of those who perform the service of authority. Even the threat of ecclesiastical punishment is, in the intention of the legislator, an exercise of charity toward those who are in error."

Despite Cardinal Malula's claim, in a press conference on November 30, that the object of the Synod was not to settle specific issues, but to shower the light of Christ on the lives of the men and women of today, this issue of the comprehension of love in communion of the church hierarchical as well as parochial, had been cavalierly avoided by the synodal participants.

In its attempt to define *aggiornamento,* Pope John's favorite expression for the updating of the Church, the final *relatio* spoke of its significance for "a missionary openness for the integral salvation of the world. Through this, all truly human values not only are accepted but energetically defended: the dignity of the human person, fundamental human rights, peace, freedom from oppression, poverty and injustice." Everything but love.

Nevertheless in its finale, the document said:

> In the end, may there come in our day that "new Pentecost" of which Pope John XXIII had spoken and which we, with all the faithful, await from the Holy Spirit. May the Spirit, through the intercession of Mary, mother of the Church, ensure that, in these last days of our century, "the Church in the world of God might celebrate the mysteries of Christ for the salvation of that world."

Bibliographical Note

Indispensible to an understanding of Synod 85 is a knowledge of what happened at Vatican Council II together with a grasp of its sixteen documents. For the English speaking world this information is contained in the compendium of the four volumes by Xavier Rynne written out of Letters from Vatican City in the *New Yorker* and published by Farrar, Strauss and Giroux as *Vatican II* (New York, 1968). An authoritative English version of the Council's Constitutions, Decrees and Declarations with commentaries was published by W. Abbott and J. Gallagher as *Documents of Vatican II* (America Press, New York, 1966. For an introduction to the origins of the Roman Synods of Bishops, there is *A New Sound in Rome: Synod '67* by G. MacEoin and F. Murphy (Milwaukee, 1968).

Of the several books that appeared in immediate preparation for the Synod the interview with Cardinal Joseph Ratzinger, prefect of the Congregation for the Doctrine of the Faith, by Mario Missiroli and published as *The Ratzinger Report* (Ignatius Press, San Francisco, 1985) made the greatest impact on supporters and critics of Vatican preparations for the Synod.

Two other volumes likewise had impact: Giancarlo Zizola's *La restaurazione di papa Wojtyla* (Laterza, Rome, 1985) and Gian Franco Svidercoschi's *Inchiesta sul Concilio* (Città Nova, Rome 1985). Zizola's book is a severe critique of the pontificate of the Polish pope as an attempt to roll back the Church to the preconciliar age despite John Paul's insistence that he is totally dedicated to implementing that assembly's teaching. Svidercoschi's volume is a collection of 29 interviews originally published in *Il Tempo* with some forty-eight personalities either immediately connected with the Council such as cardinals Suenens, Garrone and Koenig or involved in its implementation. A small volume of eighty-eight pages — *A venti anni dal Concilio: esperienze e prospettive* (Twenty years after the Council, experiences and prospectives) published by *Città Nova* contains the reminiscences of the ninety-four year old Cardinal Pietro Parente one of the principal curial protagonists at that event.

Apparently in direct response to the Ratzinger interview, the octogenarian, recently retired cardinal of Vienna, Franz Koenig allowed himself to be interviewed and the result published by Gianni Licheri as *Chiesa dove vai?*: Church, where are you going? (Borla, Rome, 1985). One of the leading lights at the Council and, by his own admission, a man highly responsible for engineering the election of Karol Wojtyla as Pope John Paul II, the Austrian cardinal gives a frank evaluation of the Ratzinger program and finds it highly wanting.

Articles in journals and periodicals, both religious and secular did much to highlight the preparations for the Synod during the ten months of its gestation.

Citations and quotations from the synodal documents and interventions are taken for the most part from the daily bulletins issued by the Holy See's Press Office, the English version of the *L' Osservatore Romano* (December 16 and 23-30) or translated from the Italian edition, as well as from the *Tablet* of London, and other papers and periodicals. All the major dailies had representatives on hand as did a large portion of the Catholic religious press. Despite criticisms and claims to the contrary, the Synod proved a newsworthy event and was so reported.

The Synod ended in a euphoric mood. In response to the papal challenge, it recaptured a sense of the élan of the council. It devloped a politique of its own whereby divergent viewpoints were gradually synthesized into a series of proposals that, with Pope John Paul II's acceptance, could propel the church prophetically into the third millennium.

Appendix I

Message to the People of God

I

We bishops, having come together from five continents and assembled in Rome for the synod with the Pope, have lived with intensity a privileged moment of communion in prayer, dialogue and study. You know, dear brothers and sisters, that the Holy Father invited us during theses days to recall with him the second Vatican Council, to evaluate its implementation, to promote it in the Church that it might be fully lived.

All of us, bishops of the Oriental rites and the Latin rite, have shared unanimously, in a spirit of thanksgiving, the conviction that the second Vatican Council is a gift of God to the Church and to the world. In full adherence to the council, we see in it a wellspring offered by the Holy Spirit to the Church, for the present and the future. We do not fix upon the errors, confusions and defects which, because of sin and human weakness, have been the occasion of suffering in the midst of the people of God. We firmly believe, and we see, that the Church finds today in the Council the light and strength that Christ has promised to give to his followers in each period of history.

II

The message of Vatican II proposes to us for our time "the inexhaustible riches of the mystery of Christ". Through the

Church which is his body, Christ is ever present in the midst of humanity. We are called, through faith and the sacraments, to live fully communion with God. Inasmuch as it is communion with the living God, Father, Son and Holy Spirit, the Church is, in Christ, the "mystery" of the love of God present in the history of mankind. The council has powerfully recalled this and we adhere to it in faith.

This is the reality that is lived and participated in by the baptized. They are members of the one body of Christ, in which the Holy Spirit abides and acts. The structures and relations within the Church must express this communion.

The first chapter of the constitution on the Church (*Lumen Gentium*) does not bear the title "Mystery of the Church" without good reason. We are speaking here of a reality of which we must be ever more certain. We are aware that the Church cannot renew itself without more profoundly rooting this spiritual note of mystery in the hearts of Christians. This note has as its first characteristic element the universal call to holiness, addressed to all the faithful as well as to those who, according to their state in life, follow the evangelical counsels. It is thus necessary to understand the profound reality of the Church, and consequently to avoid false sociological or political interpretations of the nature of the Church. In this way we will go forward without ceasing in our work, in faith and hope, for Christian unity. The Lord Jesus Christ, who is the same yesterday, today and tomorrow, assures the life and unity of the Church throughout the ages. Through this Church God offers an anticipation and a promise of the communion to which he calls all mankind.

III

Animated by this joyful hope for the Church and the world, we invite you to know better and more fully the second Vatican Council, to intensify its deepened study, to understand better the unity and the richness of all the constitutions, decrees and declarations. It is also a question of putting them more deeply into practice: in communion with

Christ present in the Church (*Lumen Gentium*), in listening to the Word of God (*Dei Verbum*), in the service of mankind, especially of the poor (*Gaudium et Spes*). The message of Vatican II, like that of the councils which have marked the history of the Church, cannot bring forth its fruits except through a sustained and persevering effort. This message must be listened to still more, with an open and willing heart. We call on you to join in our effort. We too have committed ourselves to using all the means at our disposal to help you respond to all the appeals that the council addresses to the Church. It is with particular affection that we ask priests to strive with us, for the Lord has called them to serve the people of God with us.

Every baptized man and woman, according to his or her state in life and in the Church, receives the mission to proclaim the Good News of salvation for man in Jesus Christ. Each is therefore called to exercise his or her particular responsibility. Likewise, every community is called to study deeply the concrete exigencies of the mystery of the Church and of its communion. So true is this that the Church first of all receives for itself the love and communion which it is its mission to announce to the world. The courage and discernment required today for the evangelization of the world can draw their light and dynamism from the second Vatican Council.

IV

Brothers and sisters, in the Church we experience with you, in an intense and vital way, mankind's present crises and dramas, upon which we have reflected at length. Why? In the first place, because the second Vatican Council had done so. The Council, in effect, had been convoked in order to promote the renewal of the Church with a view to evangelizing a radically changed world. Today we feel impelled towards a deeper understanding of the true significance of Vatican II, in order to respond to the world's new challenges and to those which Christ ever addresses to the world. And this, whether it be a question of challenges of the social, economic or political order, or those related to lack of respect for human life, the suppression of civil and religious liberties, contempt for the rights of families, racial discrimination, economic imbalance, insurmountable debts and the problems of international security, and the race for more powerful and terrible arms. The world's ills also stem from man's incapacity to dominate his conquests when he closes in upon himself.

From Vatican II the Church received with certitude a new light: the joy and hope which come from God can help mankind already on this earth to overcome every sadness and anguish, if men lift their gaze to the heavenly city. We hope to be able to communicate to you what we ourselves have received from this synod.

During these days of meetings and of dialogue, we share even more intensely the burden of man's sufferings. Through each bishop we are directly united in solidarity with every nation, and thus with each of you. Still, because it carries in its heart the love of Christ, dead and risen, the message of Vatican II presents with new vigor for our day the hope of the Gospel. Once again we repeat it. And through you we say it to all the men and women of our day, with humility but certitude: "We are not made for death but for life. We are not condemned to divisions and wars but called to fraternity and peace. God did not create man for hate and distrust; rather, he is made to love God. He is made for God himself. Man responds to this vocation by renewing his heart. For mankind there is a path — and we already see the signs of it — which leads to a civilization of sharing, solidarity and love; to the only civilization worthy of man. We propose to work with all of you towards the realization of this civilization of love, which is God's design for humanity as it awaits the coming of the Lord."

While fraternally encouraging you to travel this path we already direct our gaze towards the synod of 1987 on "The Vocation and Mission of the Laity of the Church and the World, Twenty Years after Vatican II". This synod concerns the whole Church: bishops, priests, deacons, men and women religious, the laity. It must also mark a decisive stage towards the reception of the grace of Vatican II on the part of all Catholics.

We invite you to prepare yourselves in your particular Churches. In this way we will all live our Christian vocation and our common mission according to the dynamism of the council.

At the conclusion of this gathering the synod gives thanks, from the depths of our hearts, to God the Father, through his Son, in the Holy Spirit, for the great grace of this century which was the second Vatican Council. It also gives thanks for the spiritual experience of this twentieth anniversary celebration. As he taught the apostles gathered with Mary in the Cenacle, so the Holy Spirit teaches us what He wishes to say to the Church on its pilgrimage towards the third millennium.

May the Spirit grant that in this century, with the intercession of Mary, "the Church be able to celebrate the mysteries of Christ for the salvation of the world."

Appendix II

The Final Report

I. The Synodal Theme: Vatican Council II Reaffirmed

(1) The spiritual experience

As this second Extraordinary Synod comes to an end, we must offer thanks to the goodness of God, who led the Supreme Pontiff to summon this synod. We are grateful to the Holy Father, Pope John Paul II, for calling us to this celebration of the twentieth anniversary of the conclusion of the second Vatican Council. The synod itself has given us the opportunity to experience our communion in the one Spirit, the one faith and hope, and in one Catholic Church; and in our common will to bring the council into the practice and life of the Church. Among ourselves we have shared joy and hope; but also the griefs and pain that the Church throughout the world often suffers.

(2) Achievement

This synod was summonded to celebrate, reaffirm and carry forward the work of the second Vatican Council. We are grateful that, with God's help, we have achieved these aims. We have celebrated Vatican II wholeheartedly, as a grace of God and gift of the Holy Spirit, from which many spiritual benefits have flowed for the universal Church, for particular Churches and for the people of our time. In the same spirit and with joy we have affirmed the meaning of Vatican II as a lawful and valid expression and interpretation of the deposit of faith contained in sacred Scripture and in the living tradition of the Church. For this reason we decided to go forward on the path that the council indicated. There was full agreement among us on the necessity of carrying forward the understanding and application of the council, both in letter and in spirit. In this way there will be fresh progress in the acceptance of the council, both in its spiritual interiorization and its practical application.

(3) Acceptance of the council

Despite incidental opposition from a small minority, by far the majority of the faithful gave Vatican II a very warm welcome. There is no doubt that the council was welcomed with heartfelt gratitude, because the Holy Spirit so encouraged his Church. Outside the Catholic Church, many people looked at the council with great interest.

Yet although great benefits have been gained since the council ended, we sincerely acknowledge failures and difficulties in implementing the council during this period. In the post-conciliar years, faulty understanding, unwise applications of the council, and other causes cast their shadow over the post-conciliar period. However, in no way can it be stated that everything that has occurred since the council has occurred because of the council.

In the so-called First World especially, one needs to ask why, after extensive and deep teaching about the Church, there often appears to be disaffection towards the Church, even though the benefits of the council abound in this area. But where the Church is oppressed by a totalitarian ideology, or where the Church raises its voice against social injustice, it appears to be accepted in a more positive way. However it cannot be denied that there, too, not all the faithful identify with the Church and with its primary mission.

(4) Sources of difficulty

In many parts of the world the Church lacks the material and human means to fulfil its mission. Not infrequently it is prevented by external constraints in the exercise of its freedom. In the rich nations, an ideology boastful of its technical potential leads to the continual increase of immanentism that brings the false worship of material profit (so-called consumerism). The result of this can be a certain blindness to spiritual realities and values. Nor can one deny the existence of forces working in society and possessing powerful influence, that act with enmity against the Church. All these things demonstrate that "the prince of this world" and "the mystery of iniquity" are still at work in our time.

Other sources of difficulty are the partial and selective reading of the council and a superficial interpretation of its teaching. On the one hand, a selective reading of the council has led to grave misunderstandings; on the other a restricted reading of the council has caused a one-sided presentation of the Church as a merely institutional structure, deprived of its mystery. Perhaps we are not free from all responsibility for the fact that young people, in particular, regard the Church critically as a mere institution. Have we not put the idea into their heads by talking too much about reforming external church structures and too little about God and Christ? At times, too, a lack of the discernment of spirits has failed to distinguish between a legitimate opening of the council to the world and the acceptance of a secularized mentality and system of values.

(5) Acceptance of the council

Such defects and others show the need of a more profound acceptance of the council. This requires four steps: a broader and deeper knowledge of the council, its internal assimilation, a loving affirmation and bringing it to life. Interior assimilation and translation into life are the only way to ensure that the council documents come alive and produce life.

Theological interpretation of the council's teaching should keep in mind all the documents and their interconnection, thus to give an accurate account of the integral meaning of the council's decisions, which are often very complex. Special attention should be paid to the four major constitutions of the council, which are the keys to the interpretation of its decrees and declarations. It is wrong to separate the pastoral character from the doctrinal force of the documents, just as it is unlawful to divide the spirit and the letter of the council. There should be more understanding of how the council is in continuity with the great tradition of the Church; and we must at the same time receive light from the council's teaching for the Church of today and the people of our time. The Church is one and the same in all councils.

(6) Suggestions

It is suggested that a pastoral plan be drawn up in individual Churches for the next few years, to ensure a wider and deeper knowledge and acceptance of the council. This will best be achieved by renewed distribution of the documents themselves and the publication of studies explaining them and making them more intelligible to the faithful. In the on-going formation of priests and those who are preparing for the priesthood, in the formation of religious, both men and women, and of all the faithful, the council's teaching should be presented to them regularly and in a way adapted to their needs through conferences and courses. Diocesan synods and other ecclesial assemblies can be very useful for the application of the council. Use of the mass media is recommended. For an accurate understanding and application of the council's teaching, it will be very useful to read and put into practice the various apostolic exhortations that are the fruit of the ordinary synods held from 1969.

II. Particular themes of the synod

A. THE MYSTERY OF THE CHURCH

(1) Secularism and the sacred

The short space of 20 years that separates us from the council has brought changes at an ever-increasing speed in human history. So the signs of the times today do not altogether coincide with the circumstances surrounding the council. The phenomenon of secularism demands special attention. The council affirmed the legitimate autonomy of temporal affairs (cf *Gaudium et Spes* 36 and elsewhere). Properly understood in this sense, secularization has to be accepted.

Quite different altogether is the secularism which consists in an autonomistic view of man and the world, a view prescinding from the dimension of mystery, neglecting or even denying it. This immanentism is a negation of the integral view of man, which leads, not to his genuine liberation, but to a new idolatry, to slavery under ideologies, to life in the narrow and often oppressive structures of this world.

In spite of secularism, there are also signs of a return to the sacred. For there are signs today of a new hunger and thirst for the transcendent and the divine. To cooperate with this return to the sacred and defeat secularism, we must open the way to the dimension of the "divine" or of mystery, and offer approaches of faith to the people of our time. As the council says, man is a question to himself, to which God alone supplies the full and final answer (cf *Gaudium et Spes* 21). Does not the spread of sects put the question to us whether at times we sufficiently cultivate a sense of the sacred?

(2) The mystery of God

The primary mission of the Church, under the impulse of the divine Spirit, is to proclaim and bear witness to the good and joyful news of God's choice, mercy and love, shown in the history of salvation and which reach their completion in the fulness of time through Jesus Christ. It's object is to communicate them to mankind as salvation by the power of the Holy Spirit. Christ is the light of the nations! By proclaiming the Gospel the Church must ensure that this light shines forth clearly. (cf *Lumen Gentium* 1). The Church becomes more credible if it speaks less about itself and more and more preaches Christ crucified (cf 1 Cor. 2,2) and witnesses to him by its life. Thus the Church is a kind of sacrament. It is a sign and an instrument of communion with God and also of communion and reconciliation of people with one another. The council's description of the Church is Trinitarian and Christocentric.

Because Jesus Christ is the Son of God and the new Adam, he reveals both the mystery of God and the mystery of man and his supreme vocation (cf *Gaudium et Spes* 22). The Son of God was made man to make men sons of God. Through this family relationship with God man is brought to his highest dignity. Hence when the Church preaches Christ, it is proclaiming salvation to mankind.

(3) The mystery of the Church

All the importance of the Church is derived from its connection with Christ. The council described the Church in various ways, as the People of God, the Body of Christ, the Bride of Christ, the Temple of the Holy Spirit, the Family of God. These descriptions of the Church are mutually complementary and must be understood in the light of the mystery of Christ or of the Church in Christ. We must not replace a false, one-sided, hierarchical notion of the Church, with a new one-sided sociological concept.

Jesus Christ is always present in his Church. In him, its eschatological character is clearly understood (cf *Lumen Gentium* Ch7). Thus the piligrim Church on earth is a messianic people (cf *Lumen Gentium* 9), which in itself anticipates the new creation. However, the Church continues to embrace sinners within itself, for it is both holy and always in need of purification, journeying on through the world's persecutions and the consolations of God towards the kingdom to come (cf *Lumen Gentium* 8). Thus the mystery of the Cross and the mystery of the Resurrection are always present together in the Church.

(4) The call to holiness

Because the Church in Christ is a mystery, it must be thought of as a sign and instrument of holiness. Hence the council taught the call of all the faithful to holiness (cf *Lumen Gentium* Ch5). The call to holiness is an invitation to a profound conversion of heart, to a share in the life of God,One and Triune,something that signifies and surpasses the fulfilment of all man's desires. Precisely in these days when many people experience an interior emptiness and a feeling of spiritual crisis, the Church must preserve and encourage a strong sense of penance, prayer, adoration, of sacrifice and self-oblation, of charity and of justice.

Throughout the history of the Church, in its most difficult circumstances, saintly men and women, have been the primary source of renewal. We badly need saints today and should earnestly pray to God for them. The institutes of consecrated life through the evangelical counsels should be aware of their special mission in today's Church, and should be encouraged in that mission. Apostolic movements, and the new "movements of spirituality", that remain in proper communion with the Church, present great hope. Lay people should play their part in the Church and in everyday life in the family, at work, in secular affairs and in their leisure, so as to penetrate and transform the world by the light and life of Christ. Rightly understood and put into practice, popular devotions are useful as nourishment for the sanctification of the people. They deserve greater attention from pastors.

For all Christians the blessed Virgin Mary, who is our Mother in the order of grace (cf *Lumen Gentium* 61) is an example of holiness and of total response to the call of God (cf *Lumen Gentium* Ch 8).

(5) Suggestions

There is great need today for the pastors of the Church to be outstanding in their witness to holiness. The program of formation in seminaries and religious houses should ensure that candidates are educated not only intellectually, but spiritually; they should be given a serious introduction to daily spiritual life (prayer, meditation, reading of Scripture, the sacraments of penance and the Eucharist). Following the mind of the decree *Presbyterorum Ordinis,* they should be trained for priestly ministry in such a way as to find in the exercise of pastoral charity, food for their own spiritual life (cf *Presbyterorum Ordinis* 16). They will be fit then to offer sound advice to the faithful for their spiritual life as they minister to them. A genuine renewal of the institutions of professed religious life should be encouraged. But so, too, should the spirituality of lay people, which is founded in their baptism. The spiritual life of married people, based on the sacrament of matrimony, demands special support and is of greatest importance in the work of passing on the faith to future generations.

B. SOURCES OF THE CHURCH'S LIFE

(a) The Word of God

(1) Scripture, tradition, the magisterium

The Church as it reverently listens to the Word of God is sent to proclaim it faithfully (cf *Dei Verbum* 1). So the preaching of the Gospel is a pre-eminent task of the Church and especially of the bishops, a task of the greatest importance today (cf *Lumen Gentium* 25). It is in this context that one sees the importance of the greatly neglected dogmatic constitution *Dei Verbum,* that was highlighted by Pope Paul VI in the apostolic exhortation *Evangelii Nuntiandi* (1974) in a more profound and up-to-date presentation.

A selective reading of this constitution is to be avoided. Above all, the search for the original meaning of sacred

Scripture, which was earnestly recommended by the council (cf *Dei Verbum* 12), cannot be separated from the living tradition of the Church (cf *Dei Verbum* 9), nor from the authentic interpretation of the Church's magisterium (*Dei Verbum* 10). The false distinction between doctrinal and pastoral office must be avoided and supressed. Indeed, pastoral purpose consists in making actual and concrete the truth of salvation, valid for all time. Bishops, as true shepherds, must show the right path to their flock, strengthen their faith and keep dangers away.

(2) Evangelization

The mystery of divine life which the Church shares must be proclaimed to all peoples. The Church is missionary by its very nature (cf *Ad Gentes* 2). Thus bishops are not only teachers of the faithful, but also heralds of the faith who bring new followers to Christ (cf *Lumen Gentium* 25). Evangelization is the first duty, not only for bishops, but also for priests and deacons, and indeed for all the faithful.

Everywhere in the world today, the transmission of the faith and of the moral values derived from the Gospel to the next generation (youth) is endangered. Knowledge of the faith and recognition of a moral order are often reduced to a minimum. A new effort is required in evangelization and in integral and systematic catechesis.

Evangelization belongs not only to mission in the ordinary sense, that is to the peoples of the world in general. Evangelization of non-believers presupposes the self-evangelization of the baptised, and also, in a way, of deacons, priests and bishops themselves.

Evangelization is made by means of witnesses; but a witness testifies, not just by words but by his own life. We must not forget that the Greek word for witness is "martyrdom" (*martyrion).* In this respect, the older Churches can learn a great deal from the new Churches, from their dynamism, their life, and their witness even to shedding of blood.

(3) Magisterium of the bishops and theologies

According to the well-known definition of St. Anselm, theology is "faith seeking understanding". Since all the faithful must give a reason for the hope that is in them (cf 1 Pet 3. 15), theology, particularly today, is needed in the life of the Church. We gladly acknowledge what has been done since the council by the theologians to expound its documents, to ensure their faithful interpretation and fruitful application. On the other hand, we regret that theological discussions have sometimes been the cause of confusion among the faithful. Closer exchange and dialogue between bishops and theologians are required for a building-up and deeper understanding of the faith.

(4) Suggestions

There is a strong general desire for a catechism or compendium of Catholic doctrine, both faith and morals, which could be a point of reference for the catechisms or compendiums composed in various regions of the Church. The manner of doctrinal presentation should be biblical and liturgical, offering sound teaching adapted to the life of Christians today.

Training for the priesthood must be given the greatest care. There must be instruction in philosophy and theology should be taught according to the decree *Optatam totius.*

Manuals are recommended provided they offer a theology that is sound and expressed in a scientific style on good pedagogical principles that convey a genuine sense of the Church.

(b) Sacred Liturgy

(1) Internal renewal of the liturgy

The liturgical renewal is the most visible fruit of the whole work of the council. Though there were some difficulties, in general it was joyfully and fruitfully accepted by the faithful.

Liturgical reform cannot be restricted to ceremonies, rites, texts, and so on. Active participation, so happily increased since the council, consists not only in external activity, but first of all in interior and spiritual participation, a lively and fruitful sharing in the paschal mystery of Christ (cf *Sacrum Concilium* 11). The liturgy, if anything, must nourish and illumine the sense of the sacred. It should be filled with the spirit of reverence, of giving worhip and glory to God.

(2) Suggestions

Bishops should not only correct abuses but also explain clearly for their people the theological foundation of sacramental practice and of the liturgy.

Catechesis should again be the method of introduction to liturgical life, as it was in the early Church (*catecheses mystagogicae*).

Future priests should learn the liturgical life by experience and should have a good knowledge of the theology of the liturgy.

C. THE CHURCH AS COMMUNION

(1) The meaning of communion

The ecclesiology of communion is a central and fundamental idea in the documents of the council. *Koinonia*/communion, based on sacred Scripture, was held in great honour in the ancient Church and is so held in the Eastern Churches right up to our time. Since Vatican II much has been done to make the Church, as communion, more clearly understood and more concretely translated into living reality.

What does the complex word "communion" mean? Fundamentally, it is a matter of our communion with God through Jesus Christ in the Holy Spirit. This communion exists through the Word of God and the sacraments. Baptism is the door and foundation of the Church's communion; the Eucharist is the source of the whole of Christian life and its summit (*Gentium* 11). Communion with the Body of Christ in the Eucharist signifies and brings about, or builds up, the intimate union of all the faithful in the Body of Christ, which is the Church (cf 1 Cor 10, 16 *seq*).

The Ecclesial understanding of communion cannot be reduced to a matter of organization or questions concerning power. Ecclesiological communion is the foundation for order in the Church, and especially for the correct relation between unity and pluriformity.

(2) Unity and pluriformity

Just as we believe in one God, in one only mediator Jesus Christ, in one Spirit, we have also one baptism and one Eucharist, by which the unity and uniqueness of the Church are signified and built up. This is of special importance in our time, because the Church, as one and unique, is a kind of sacrament. It is a sign and instrument of unity, of reconciliation and peace among people, nations, classes and races. By the unity of faith and sacraments, and by its hierarchic unity, especially with the center of unity given to us by Christ in the office of Peter, the Church is that messianic people of which the constitution *Lumen Gentium* (9) speaks. Ecclesial communion with Peter and his successor is not an obstacle to, but an anticipation and prophetic sign of, a fuller unity.

On the other hand, one and the same Spirit is at work in many different spiritual gifts and charisms (cf 1 Cor 12, 4 *seq*); one and the same Eucharist is celebrated in various places. For this reason the one universal Church is in all the particular Churches (cf *Christus Dominus* 11). They are formed in the likeness of the universal Church; so that the one unique Catholic Church exists in and from the particular Churches (cf *Lumen Gentium* 23). Here we have the true theological principle of variety and pluriformity in unity, pluriformity to be distinguished from mere pluralism. Pluriformity is a genuine richness and involves a completion, it is true catholicity; but the pluralism of deeply opposed factions leads to dissolution and destruction and the loss of identity.

(3) The Eastern Churches

Because of its understanding of communion, the Catholic Church today has a high regard for the institutions, liturgical rites, church traditions and discipline of Christian life of the Eastern Churches. They are outstanding for their venerable antiquity and because there is in them a tradition coming from the apostles through the fathers (cf *Orientalium Ecclesiarum* 1). From most ancient times, the patriarchate has been firmly established among them, and was recognized by the first councils (cf *Ecclesiae Orientales* 7). Moreover, the Eastern Churches have borne witness for Christ and his Church by the blood of their martyrs.

(4) Collegiality

The ecclesiology of the church as communion provides a sacramental foundation for collegiality. So the theology of collegiality provides a far more extensive way of understanding the church than could a mere juridical consideration. A collegial spirit is wider than collegiality understood only in a juridical sense. Collegial spirit is the soul of collaboration between bishops whether in the regional, national or international field.

Collegial action in the strict sense implies the activity of the whole college, together with its head, directed toward the whole Church; its obvious expression is in an ecumenical council. In the theological question of the relationship between the primacy and the college of bishops, a distinction cannot be made between the Roman Pontiff and the bishops taken collectively, but between the Roman Pontiff separately and the Roman Pontiff together with the bishops (cf *Lumen Gentium*, explanatory note 3); because the college, together with its head and never without this head, is the subject of supreme and full power over the universal Church (cf *Lumen Gentium* 22).

One must distinguish between collegiality taken in the strict sense and various partial realizations, which are truly the sign and instrument of collegial spirit: the Synod of Bishops, bishops' conferences, the Roman Curia, *ad limina* visits, and so on. Not all of these realizations flow from the theological principle of collegiality; but all are governed by church law. However, they and other forms, like the pastoral journeys of the Holy Father are a service of great importance for the whole College of Bishops, together with the Pope, and also for the individual bishops whom the Holy Spirit has appointed to rule over the Church of God (cf Acts 20, 28).

(5) Conference of bishops

The collegial spirit is carried to concrete application by the conferences of bishops (cf *Lumen Gentium* 23). No one can doubt their pastoral usefulness, indeed their necessity in present-day circumstances. In the conferences of bishops, the bishops of the same nation or territory exercise their pastoral office jointly (cf *Christus Dominus* 38; CIC can 447).

In the procedure of the bishops' conferences there should be kept in view the good of the Church, the service of unity, and the inalienable responsibility of each bishop towards the universal Church and his own individual Church.

(6) Sharing in the Church

Because the Church is a communion, there must be sharing and coresponsibility at all levels. This general principle has to be understood differently in different settings.

Between the bishop and his presbyterate there exists a relationship based on the sacrament of order. So the priests in each locality in a way make the bishop present to their congregations, take up his duties and his concern so far as they can, and exercise them with daily pastoral care (cf *Lumen Gentium* 28). Therefore there should be friendly and fully trusting relationships between the bishop and his priests. Bishops feel a sense of gratitude towards their priests, who have played a large part in putting the council into practice during the post-conciliar period (cf *Optatam Totius* 1); the bishops wish to be close to their priests as far as possible, and to provide support and assistance to them in their frequently difficult labours, particularly in their parishes.

The spirit of collaboration with deacons, and also between the bishop and religious men and women working in his particular Church should be encouraged.

Since Vatican II, a new type of collaboration between lay people and clergy has happily come about in the Church. The spirit of readiness in which a great number of lay people have offered themselves for the service of the Church must be counted among the benefits of the council. In this they are the Church.

There has been question in these last years of the vocation and mission of women in the Church. The Church should see that women take their place in the Church in such a way that they can adequately use their proper gifts for the service of the Church, and have a more extensive part in the various fields of the Church's apostolate (cf *Apostolicam Actuositatem* 9). Pastors should gratefully take up and encourage the collaboration of women in the work of the Church.

The council calls young people the hope of the Church (cf *Gravissimum Educationis* 2). This synod turns to young people with a special love and with great confidence, and looks for much from their generous dedication, urging them to take their place in the mission of the Church and thereby take up and promote dynamically the inheritance of the council.

Because the Church is a communion, the new so-called "basic communities", if they genuinely live in the unity of the Church, are a true expression of communion and an instrument for fashioning a more profound communion. They thus offer great hope for the life of the Church (cf *Evangelii Nuntiandi* 58).

(7) Ecumenical communion

Relying on the ecclesiology of communion, the Catholic Church at the time of Vatican II fully assumed its ecumenical responsiblity. After these 20 years we can assert that ecumenism is deeply and indelibly inscribed on the consciousness of the Church. We bishops ardently desire that the incomplete communion with non-Catholic Churches and communities that now exists may, with the help of God's grace, reach full communion.

Ecumenical dialogue must be carried on in diffxchange of prayer. The dialogue is authentic and fruitful if it presents the truth with love and with fidelity to the Church. In this way ecumenical dialogue causes the Church to be seen more clearly as the sacrament of unity. Although communion between Catholics and other Christians is incomplete, it calls all to collaborate in many areas, and thus renders possible in some ways a common witness to the salvific love of God for the world that needs salvation.

(8) Suggestions

(a) The new Code of Canon Law, so happily promulgated, is of great help in the application of the council for the Latin Church: the wish is on this account expressed that the eastern codification be brought to completion as soon as possible.

(b) Since bishops' conferences are so useful, indeed necessary in the present pastoral work of the Church, a study of their theological standing is desired, and especially a clearer and more profound explanation of their doctrinal authority, keeping in mind the content of the council's decree *Christus Dominus* (38), and of canons 447 and 753 in the Code of Canon Law.

(c) A study is recommended of the question whether the principle of subsidiarity that has force in human society can be applied in the Church, and at what level and in what sense such application could or ought to take place (cf Pius XII, AAS 38, 1946, p 144).

D. THE MISSION OF THE CHURCH IN THE WORLD

(1) Importance of the Constitution *Gaudium et Spes*

The Church as a communion is a sacrament for the salvation of the world. Therefore powers in the Church have been granted by Christ for the world's salvation. In this context we assert the great importance and great actuality of the pastoral constitution *Gaudium et Spes*. At the same time we are aware that the signs of the times now are somewhat different from those existing at the time of the council, with an increase of problems and suffering. Everywhere today there is a growing amount of hunger, oppression, injustice and war, of torture and terrorism and other forms of violence of every kind. This demands a new and deeper theological reflection to interpret such signs in the light of the Gospel.

(2) The theology of the Cross

In today's difficulties it seems to us that God wants us to teach at a deeper level the value, importance and centrality of the Cross of Jesus Christ. Hence the relationship between human history and the history of salvation should be explained in the light of the paschal mystery. The theology of the Cross in no way excludes the theology of creation and incarnation, but, as is obvious, presupposes it. When we Christians speak about the Cross, we do not deserve the accusation of pessimism, for we are founded on the realism of Christian hope.

(3) *Aggiornamento*

In this paschal perspective that asserts the unity of Cross and Resurrection, one discerns the true and the false sense of the term *aggiornamento*. It excludes the merely facile adjustment that would lead to the secularisation of the Church. Also excluded is a rigid closing of the community of the faithful upon itself. What is affirmed is a missionary expansion for the integral salvation of the world. Through this all truly human values are not only accepted but bravely defended: the dignity of the human person; fundamental rights of mankind, peace, freedom from oppression, misery and injustice. Integral salvation, however, is obtained only if these human realities are purified and further raised by grace to familiarity with God through Jesus Christ in the Holy Spirit.

(4) Inculturation

Here, too, we have a theological principle for the problem of inculturation. Since the Church is a communion, which joins diversity and unity, being present throughout the world it accepts whatever it finds positive in all cultures. Inculturation, however, is different from a mere external adaptation. It signifies an interior transformation of authentic cultural values through integration into Christianity, and the rooting of Christianity in the various human cultures.

A split between the Gospel and culture is called by Pope Paul VI 'a harmful accident of our time.' We need to make every effort for the careful evangelization of human culture or rather of the cultures themselves. They must be reborn from their union with the Good News. However, this union will not come about if the Good News is not proclaimed" (*Evangelii Nuntiandi* 20).

(5) Dialogue with non-Christian Religions and non-believers

Vatican II stated that the Catholic Church does not reject anything that is true and holy in non-Christian religions. Indeed it encourages Catholics through conversation and collaboration prudently and charitably made with followers of other religions, while witnessing to their own faith and Christian life, to acknowledge, preserve and foster the spiritual and moral goods and socio-cultural values found among them (cf *Nostra Aetate* 2). The council also affirmed that God does not refuse the possibility of salvation to any individual of good will (cf *Lumen Gentium* 16). The possibilities in practice of dialogue in various regions depend on concrete circumstances. All these points are valid in dialogue with non-believers.

Dialogue should not be set in opposition to mission. Authentic dialogue's purpose is for the human person to open and communicate his interior self to the person with whom he is conversing. Furthermore, all Christians have received from Christ the mission to make all peoples disciples of Christ himself (cf Matt 28, 18). God can use dialogue between Christians and non-Christians or non-believers as a way to communicate the fullness of grace.

(6) Preferential option for the poor

After Vatican II, the Church became more aware of her mission for service of the poor, the oppressed and the marginalized. In this preferential option, which is not to be understood as exclusive, the true spirit of the Gospel shines out. Jesus Christ declared the poor blessed (cf Matt 5,3; Lk 6,20) and himself willed to be poor for our sake (cf 2 Cor 8,9).

Besides poverty of material goods, there is also an absence of freedom and of spiritual goods which can be called, in a way, a form of poverty, and which is especially serious when religious freedom is suppressed by force.

The Church must in prophetic fashion denounce every form of poverty and oppression and defend and support everywhere the fundamental and inalienable rights of the human person. This is of greatest importance when there is question of protecting human life right from the beginning, protecting it from aggressors in all circumstances and truly supporting it in every respect.

The synod expresses its communion with its brothers and sisters who are suffering persecution for their faith and their support of justice, and prays earnestly for them to God.

We must understand as integral the Church's saving mission in relation to the world. Although the Church's mission is spiritual, it involves promotion of human progress even in the temporal field.

For this reason the Church's mission is not reduced to a single faceted movement in whatever sense that may be understood. In its mission there is certainly a distinction, but in no way a separation between the aspects of nature and those of grace. This duality is not dualism. False and useless oppositions as, for example, between spiritual mission and service for the world are to be discarded and ignored.

(7) Suggestions

As the world is in a state of continual evolution, we must analyze the signs of the times over and over again, so that the message of the Gospel may be heard more clearly and the Church's activity for the salvation of the world may become more intense and alive. In this context we should again examine what are the following aims, and how may they be put into practice:

(a) the theology of the Cross and the Paschal Mystery in preaching, in the sacraments and in the life of the Church of our time;

(b) the theology and practice of inculturation and dialogue with non-Christian religions and non-believers;

(c) what is a preferential option for the poor;

(d) the social doctrine of the Church in relation to human development in ever-changing circumstances.

At the end of this assembly, the synod gives heartfelt thanks to God the Father through his Son in the Holy Spirit for the greatest grace of this century, the second Vatican Council. It also give thanks for the spiritual experience of this celebration of its 20th anniversary, which has filled our hearts with joy and hope even among the pain and grief of our times. Just as He taught the apostles in the upper room with Mary, so the Holy Spirit has taught us what He wishes to say to the Church in its pilgrimage towards the third millennium.

We bishops, together with and under Peter, commit ourselves to more deeply understanding Vatican II and bringing it into the practice of the Church, as was proposed in this assembly of the synod. We have celebrated the council and reaffirmed its purpose. Let us carry forward its work. The message of the council, already received with great agreement by the whole Church, is and remains the Magna Carta for future times.

Finally may there come for our days that "new Pentecost" of which Pope John XXIII spoke, and which we, with all the faithful, await from the Holy Spirit. May the Spirit, by the intercession of Mary, Mother of the Church, ensure that as this century comes to an end "the Church subject to the Word of God may celebrate the mysteries of Christ for the salvation of the world."